WHISPERS FROM THE ANCIENT ONES

WHISPERS FROM THE ANCIENT ONES

E.C. SANDERS

JF
Creating Forward Press

Copyright

To my parents:

I am grateful for all you did for our family; and the difference you
made in the lives of those blessed to know you.

Contents

Copyright   iii

Dedication   iv

Introduction   1

Saint Francis of Assisi Prayer   3

Part One: Shadows that Seem to Shatter the Soul   4

  1 The Early Years   5

  2 The Littlest Soul   8

  3 Forgiveness   11

  4 Healing Through Forgiveness   13

  5 Deceptive Neighbor   22

  6 Taking a Stand   24

  7 The End of Innocence   27

  8 Hawaii   33

  9 The Unexpected   35

 10 My Beloved Mother   40

Part Two: Wounds to Wisdom   46

 11 The Beginning of Healing   47

 12 Learning More About Forgiveness   50

 13 Thoughts Are Physical Things   58

 14 Timeless Peace   65

15 Ho'oponopono   72

16 The Dream We Dream   80

17 Letting Go of Our Stuff   85

18 Lucid Dreaming - A Powerful Tool   90

19 Dream Signs   97

Resources   106

Additional Reading and Videos   109

Pass It On Book Series   111

About the Author   113

Introduction

I have always had a memory of asking to come here, to this holographic, seemingly physical world. A place where we forget almost all of who we truly are, where we originate from, and just how profoundly empowered we are. The indescribable love we come from, the Source of all that is- Prime Creator.

I was told, "You do not realize how difficult it will be. You have no idea." I kept asking the council to be allowed to go. A loud, clear voice called out, "Let her go. She can make a difference!" I have often wondered if this was the voice of God, the omnipresent One. If not the voice of God, then certainly a high being of love and light, or a Seraphim Angel. It seems likely it was the voice of an Elder overseeing the Council of Twelve, the overseers of this realm. I had traveled throughout many galaxies and star systems, far, far away from planet Earth. And so, I was conceived and born.

They were correct, I had no idea of what I agreed to do in coming here. I was born an empath. Not just empathic, a full-on empath. As a child, I could see a dead animal and instantly know and feel everything it experienced and went through- its thoughts, feelings; the turmoil, fear, trauma, etc. All of it rushed into my consciousness. It was disturbing for me. As an adult, I learned how to shut this off and keep it from entering my field. I eventually learned to do this with people, places, and things. I felt it all from everything. Often, I did not know how to tell what was coming from me or from something or someone else.

I offer this book to anyone seeking to find a way out of emotional discomfort and pain. May peace and healing be with you and may your path to healing be shorter and much smoother than mine was.

I ask to be forgiven by anyone I have harmed or hurt, in any way, consciously or unconsciously; intended or unintended. Through any thoughts, words, or actions.

I forgive anyone who has harmed or hurt me, in any way, intentionally or unintentionally. I decide to have peace as my first priority as I live each moment of my life.

I choose to be free of anything deterring me from my inner sanctuary. I bless every being, in all forms, living or in spirit, with harmony, peace, and love. I do my best to forgive myself when I fall short, missing the mark, so to speak.

My intention is to help others as I help myself and that I help myself as I help others. May this book be a tool for spiritual enrichment.

Saint Francis of Assisi Prayer

I have always loved this prayer from the first time I read it:

Lord, make me an instrument of Thy peace.
Where there is hatred, let me sow love.
Where there is injury, pardon.
Where there is error, truth.
Where there is doubt, faith.
Where there is despair, hope.
Where there is darkness, light.
And where there is sadness, joy.
O Divine Master, grant that I may not so much seek
to be consoled as to console.
To be understood as to understand.
To be loved as to love.
For it is in giving that we receive.
It is in pardoning that we are pardoned.
And it is in dying that we are born to eternal life.
~ Prayer of Saint Francis of Assisi

Part One: Shadows that Seem to Shatter the Soul

1

The Early Years

Growing up and in the beginning of my adult life, I identified myself with the "walking wounded." As I continued to grow, my identity became one with the warrior. I was fierce, protecting the fragile, tender inner places still waiting for healing. Anger and justification were my fuels.

Today, my identity is with the healed and empowered. It is in my journey from wounded to empowered that I share with you here on these pages. This is one woman's story of her journey of discovery in becoming empowered through forgiveness and therefore finding peace and healing. I took my life back.

I became aware of the incredible power which exists within forgiveness. I learned to become empowered by looking outside the walls of my pain and anger. This graceful force moved me beyond the discomfort and confusion, to release that which was determined to swallow me up, wholly and completely. My choice instead was to take what was agonizing and terrifying in my life and turn it around, utilizing it to fuel my own self-empowerment... to bring my heart and mind the peace needed for healing.

This book was written to help others step out of the pain they may be in and to be free of this prison. A prison, which is unknowingly self-imposed because of the pain and traumatic experiences we have gone through. Traumas keep us in captivity as we continue to carry them with us- all the while, these traumatic experiences are calling out to be healed.

In a heartfelt discussion of what to include in this book, I took the advice of one of my friends, Kathy P. She told me to "give the details of the things that caused me to reach so deeply to forgive." She went on to say, "You really need to talk about the actual experiences you have had and what you have been through."

I repeatedly replied, protesting, "I do not want to go there. I am very uncomfortable talking about those things. I want to forget about them." I also explained I had a different idea of how to glaze over the exact experiences without getting into the details.

She agreed it could be difficult for me. However, she was adamant this needed to be done. Kathy P. finally convinced me of the significance it would bring in helping others to understand the power and grace of forgiveness.

So here it is. As I make known very sensitive and painful experiences, you will realize the importance of why I have chosen to bare my soul. With this, be assured, it is conceivable for anyone willing, that they too can choose to heal.

It is possible to rise up renewed and empowered, comparable to the phoenix ascending from burned ashes. It is encouraging to know we can exchange the raw wounds for exquisite peace- the peace we all seek. This peace comes through the grace of forgiving.

2

The Littlest Soul

I first heard this story many years ago in a large, weekend seminar with Christopher Howard. I am recapping what he shared with us and adding some of my own understanding.

There is a story about the littlest soul, up in heaven, wanting to come down to earth to experience forgiveness and to make a difference. No one would give this littlest soul permission to come to earth. The littlest soul was told, "It is too dangerous. It is really difficult. You will experience a lot of pain." Finally, a big soul stepped forward and volunteered to go to Earth with the littlest soul. The littlest soul exclaimed, "Really, you will go with me?!"

Yes, I will go with you. However, you must know that you will not re-member who I am. I certainly may do terrible, seemingly unforgivable things to you. You will need to reach deep within the depths of yourself to forgive. You may think you do not know even how to begin this. You will have experiences that are completely unjust, make no sense, and will disrupt your life. However, once you do forgive, it will enable you to move forward in open-ing your mind and awareness to insights and knowledge you could not have had before. It will bring your heart and mind home to heaven by bringing you inner peace. Littlest soul, you will move to higher levels of understanding and gain enormous soul growth. You will help other people in ways you could not have known before experiencing this forgiveness. You will have to try very hard to remember your purpose of forgiveness and why you wanted to come to earth.

The littlest soul agreed, and they went down to earth to experience forgiveness.

Imagine just for a moment if we are the littlest soul and we are being asked to do our part to move forward in our soul growth- letting go of the pain and experiencing the peace.

Forgiveness is the way to peace, which is natural to our being and essential for our well-being. What if this is why we are all here, to experience forgiveness, thereby receiving peace and healing?

I believe this story, which was told to us at that seminar, came from Neale Donald Walsch's book *The Littlest Soul and the Sun.*

So, we respect the illusion,
and we find peace through forgiveness.

3

Forgiveness

Forgiveness does not, in any way, mean someone is not responsible for their transgressions or that they do not need to atone for their actions, or crimes, or receive punishment (and hopefully rehabilitate). It simply means we get to free ourselves from being tied to anger, hatred, resentment, fear, pain, etc. We receive freedom from the experience.

Forgiveness brings peace and healing. It energetically releases us from whomever or whatever we are forgiving. Forgiveness also allows healing for the other person or circumstance. It is truly what any of us really want. We desire, at the deepest part of ourselves, from our hearts, to heal, to be free, and for the offender to be healed.

We need to be gentle with ourselves. Consider that within each of us is a small child of about the age of four or five years old. We can forgive this child for anything we demanded of ourselves and have not achieved, or mistakes we have made.

Take care of your inner child. It is equally important to forgive ourselves and free ourselves from inner criticism, expectations, and disappointments. As we practice forgiveness with our self, we allow our self peace and the opportunity to heal.

4

Healing Through Forgiveness

Forgiveness is the power tool I use to understand the traumatic experiences I had in my life. It has helped heal my feelings of guilt, shame, anger, jealousy, and an inner gnawing of not being enough. Forgiveness has helped me find strength and confidence.

For ages, forgiving my father felt like an unscalable mountain. I felt guilty for expressing the pain I carried, and for saying anything negative about my dad. He was a wonderful husband, father, and provider-faithful and devoted to my mother, standing by her through many serious illnesses. He was always there for my sister and me when we needed him. Friends and neighbors admired him. He was known for driving my sister, me, and our friends just about anywhere, even taking our friends home when their parents would not. My dad always knew where we were and what we were doing, ensuring we were safe. He was present in our lives in a way many fathers were not.

My father was kind, loving, and compassionate. He worked hard and deeply valued his family. He had a natural connection with animals and nature. He was also incredibly modest, always mindful of how he carried himself around us. He made sure to knock before entering our bedroom. Even when upset and ready to discipline us, he would step back and wait if we told him we weren't dressed.

But my father also had an unpredictable temper.

Aside from spanking me and my sister when we were younger, my dad never clobbered my sister, and he never laid a hand on my mother. However, with me, it was different. My dad had large, strong hands. He often backhanded me or punch-slapped me across the face with hits hard enough to make my nose bleed. I'd lie in bed for what felt like hours, pressing an ice pack against the back of my neck, swallowing blood, waiting for the bleeding to stop. Twice, my mother took me to the doctor. Each time, the doctor cauterized a vein inside my nose, trying to stop the recurring hemorrhaging.

Since I was active and fairly hyper, the doctor suggested I get out of bed at a slower pace. He said to "sit up, wait a minute, and then stand up. Walk more rather than run." He thought I triggered my nosebleeds by sprinting out of bed and running around too much. This may have been partially true. Still, everyone seemed oblivious to the fact that Dad's blows could be the cause.

Why Dad hit me wouldn't be revealed for decades. Along with that revelation, a lineage of anger and grief would be released- back through nine generations! Total forgiveness for Dad's painful actions wouldn't come for years after that. Even with my utmost, fervent wanting, forgiveness did not grace me fully for decades. And yet, when I accepted complete forgiveness might never happen and made peace with what I had not forgiven, grace rushed in.

It happened- finally and unexpectedly- in a mediation led by Michael Mirdad. During the last Sunday service I attended when living in Sedona, Arizona, and just before moving to Hot Springs Village, Arkansas, peace flowed into my heart and mind. A beautiful, comforting wave of Spirit flowed through me, washing away the grit and jagged edges of my wounds. I felt a profound shift within my being. Providence came when I was ready and fully willing to receive.

Michael Mirdad often says to "deal with what you need to deal with here on earth while remembering to respect the illusion of being here." By being fully present for Michael's meditation, I was exclaiming to the Universe and to the Ancient Ones that I was ready to deal with my deepest wounds. Little did I know that the grace of one hundred percent forgiveness would miraculously become one with me-that I would become one with forgiveness.

There were many little miracles in the years prior, although miracles don't come in sizes. They are all the same- acts of love. Being fully present in what we may typically dismiss as little moments signals to the universe that we are open to forgiveness and healing, clearing the path for miracles to unfold.

When we accept every act of love as a miracle, we become the grace that washes away the pain.

Many years earlier, after marrying my husband, Mike, we moved to San Juan Island from Southern California. Three years later, I was strongly guided to move to Arizona. I could not have gone directly from California to Arizona. "I will never live in the desert!" I had always said. "Ha-Ha!" responded Life! Spirit has a way of getting us to where we are to be on our path. My husband was thrilled! He loves the heat and the dessert. Spirit knew it needed to move me step-by-step.

During one of our meditations, while living on San Juan Island, Washington, our guides directed Mike to conduct an extraction. Mike is a shaman and a registered Cherokee. (When I refer to God, my guides, the Ancient Ones, I am speaking of the omnipresence of the One, of Source the Absolute. For me, all works together in different forms.) A nine-generation entity was energetically poking its head out of me and was clairvoyantly shown to my husband. It had been passed from one generation to the next through the males on my dad's side, as was explained to Mike. My mother had miscarried a boy before she became pregnant with me. It passed to me instead as I was the next born.

Fortunately, I was the ninth generation and in a position to have this extraction. (It could have passed on to my sister's son instead.) We knew what to do. Our spiritual team removed this being/entity. The team arranged for it to be reunited with its kindred from another dimension. It had originally become entwined with my eighth-great grandfather when he had a traumatic experience. Over the generations, this entity festered with frustration, and its fury grew. Its grip was so strong on my father that it lashed out through him by striking me.

Growing up, rage smoldered within me, but I felt the need to keep it under control. And, after the entity/shadow being was released (in my sixties and twenty years after my dad passed), my inner inferno was vanquished. The entity was commanded to go, and it couldn't return- it was too uncomfortable with my Light. My relentless, fiery angst was doused, for it had nothing to fuel it. Decades later, I was guided to also forgive the entity. Wow! How had I missed this part of forgiveness?

I wrote about this first because I have always felt guilty saying anything against my dad. He was a wonderful man. After my dad passed, he asked me many times to please forgive him completely. He was around me spiritually for years, helping me in my life. My mother was also. Long after their passing, we are still in contact.

I adored and feared Dad at the same time. I was deeply confused about loving him growing up. My friends knew he was a strict and fierce disciplinarian, along with being kind, supportive, and trustworthy; they admired and shrank before him as well. My mother was also quite strict. I often found myself on restriction, grounded. As an adult, I realized it was their way of protecting us.

Where was my mother during the poundings? I've asked myself this many times. Perhaps her absence resulted from her upbringing. Mom was raised by a very strict, iron-willed man, from what I understand. Although he was fluent in seven languages, Granddad had more than his share of hardships. He was a Russian Jewish immigrant who literally escaped from Russia after the overthrow of the Tsar. He and unconfirmed family members hid among a cattle transporter to make it to Bremerhaven, Germany, and then took a ship to America. They left everyone and everything they knew. All of it was gone; homes and land confiscated, family and friends imprisoned, killed, or hopefully fleeing elsewhere. No one had any information as to what happened after their escape. My grandfather changed their family name, worried they would be followed and killed.

Perhaps he was a mean man. My sister sure thought so. It was mean how he treated my mom, even though he loved her deeply. Mom told me she overheard her dad talking about "how proud he was of her; how much he admired her, and how he didn't want to spoil her." Mom told me she was astonished to hear her dad say this about her. The discipline he enacted on Mom certainly made him seem to be. Strict, sometimes seemingly barbaric discipline was what my mother experienced from her father.

Mom was afraid of mice. She told us her father put her in a room with a mouse running around so she could overcome her fear. (What?!) Another example was making Mom eat eggs and saying she was just being stubborn for not eating them. Mom had a terrible time eating eggs and would even throw up. As an adult, Mom discovered she was extremely allergic to eggs.

However, my maternal grandfather was a man who loved his family and strived to provide for and protect them. Our mom spoke of her father numerous times kissing the ground and declaring how grateful he was to be living in America. She only mentioned our Russian last name to me once and wrote it down for me. Then she tore it up after showing me.

My maternal grandmother was well-educated. Her father was a principal Rabbi in Kyiv, Russia, currently in Ukraine. I imagine this makes me Russian Ukrainian. My mother adored her parents. Her mother died when my mom was about eleven. It was still painful for her to speak about this, even as an adult woman. Her father's passing when she was twenty-six was another huge emotional blow. Then, there was the great depression during her young adult life.

My mother was loving, creative, kind, generous, and a gourmet chef. She could cook and bake anything. She wrote poetry and music. She had a beautiful singing voice. She was a master organizer. Everything was exact and orderly in our closets, drawers, shelves- everywhere. There were many times she brought home someone from the church for a hot meal. My mother sometimes offered her or Dad's clothing to help a person going through a tough time. She had a specialness about her, which touched everyone who met her.

My mother was very protective of our overall care and well-being. She may have seen my father's discipline as normal, as she was a strict disciplinarian herself. Or, she may not have actually seen Dad hit me. Whatever or why, I forgave my mother a long time ago. I forgave her for not knowing to protect me from Dad. I forgave her for her silence, blind spots, and fears that froze her. I forgave her because carrying the shackles of her mistakes would drown me in my pain, keeping me from seeing the truth of my being, the truth of the Source of my being that is the Source of all healing.

Around second grade, I began remembering the Star People and wanted to reach for the stars, but spankings turned into surprise blows to my face. And I did see stars! But at the cost of getting painfully bruised and emotionally shaken. Once, Dad slapped me across my face with his open hands, slapping my face back and forth between his big hands. Another time when I was older, he sucker-punched me in my face with his fist. And another time, Dad slapped my face back and forth while walloping me between each smack.

Thankfully, I met my soul sister, CeCe, when I was in third grade. I remember sitting on the bathroom floor after my dad had smacked me around. My nose was bleeding. I was rocking myself back and forth, laughing and crying, trying to shake it off. It was the first time CeCe came over to my house and I was horribly embarrassed and shook up. She remembers seeing me like this and was speechless. She had her own dysfunctional family and rough upbringing in different ways. CeCe is one of my friends who remembers my dad hitting me. We have been close friends and like sisters since our first meeting.

I also wet the bed until I was almost thirteen. I was a deep sleeper. I was spending time with my star family and healing when I slept. I remember once waking up, standing in a corner with my mom swatting me with a fly swatter. My dad told her, "That's enough!" Dad stopped her from continuing. Mom had to wake me up at night to use the bathroom so I wouldn't wet my bed. Another time when I was younger, she slapped me across my face with the comb she was using to comb my hair. I had fine, curly, auburn red hair. It seemed to me my parents were very frustrated with me much of the time.

My dad grew up Catholic on a five-hundred-acre farm in Texas. He felt his family were the lucky ones during the depression. Living on a farm, they always had enough to eat, even though other things were scarce. At seventeen, he had his dad sign for him to join the Navy. He wanted to make something of himself. He became a naval officer with a twenty-year career.

His father's ancestry was the original family from Scotland. Much of his line moved over to Ireland around six generations back. They settled in one of the original thirteen colonies, West Virginia, in the mid-1740s. My grandfather and his family eventually traveled from West Virginia to Texas in a wagon train. We still have the family hope chest and a dresser they brought with them.

My paternal grandparents met in Texas. She was outside, sweeping in front of her father's general store. My grandfather, with his red hair and a mustache, rode up on his horse, scattering dust and debris. She did not appreciate this, in the least. It was love at first sight for him! My grandmother did not appreciate his arrival, nor did she feel the same about him. Eventually, he won her over with his kind and gentlemanly ways. My grandfather doted over my grandmother. He cherished her and his family. My grandmother's father was Polish, and her mother was a possible mix of Native American Indian, Pennsylvania Dutch, and French.

While my dad was overseas in the Navy, his parents sold the farm and moved to Austin, Texas. My grandfather did not want my dad to feel burdened or responsible for the farm. He wished for him a life of his own choosing. My dad often mentioned he wished he knew and could have done more for his parents. His parents were happy with their decision to retire from the farm.

As I grew up we usually visited our Texas family in the summer when Dad took his vacation from work. My grandparents had neighbors down the alley with a yard full of chickens. When I was three or four years old, somehow I managed to walk by myself to see the "cluck clucks" as I described them. When my grandfather found me and brought me back home to their house, he cut a branch from a tree and "switched" my legs, to teach me to never go there by myself again. Everyone there apparently accepted this as the way things were done. My father most likely learned this way from his father.

It stayed with me, though. I carried the anguish into adulthood. It may seem to be a small thing; however, for me, it was traumatic. It greatly affected my trust in my grandfather and how I felt about him from then on. It jarred my feelings of being safe. I felt unheard by the very people who were supposed to be my caregivers. I felt unsafe around the very people who were supposed to be my loved ones.

It took a long time and a lot of forgiveness work for my inner child to fully forgive my grandfather. Then, I was finally able to clear it. Once I did, I was free of it and so was he. How many people can you free today?

5

Deceptive Neighbor

In the 1950s, at about the age of eight, I was molested twice by a neighbor. My parents were watching us from a window, as this neighbor, neighborhood kids, other adults, and I played tag football in the courtyard grass next door. It seemed innocent to my parents. But how could they miss the male neighbor throwing himself toward me, falling on top of me, and rubbing himself on me? How could they ignore me fighting to get up?!

I told my parents what happened. They said I was exaggerating or getting things confused. The tag football game seemed like a simple stumble and pile-up to them. Only it was not! I felt that weird man's penis through his pants and on my crotch and then my legs. There was no mistake. He didn't just get up or roll over right away to get off of me. He stayed there and rubbed himself on me, long enough for me to know something wasn't right.

Even if I was wrong about that experience, the second time was loud and clear!

On his second attempt, he grabbed my arm and pulled me into a nearby garage, then yanked me over to him. He tried to fondle me. I strained to pull away, and he held me tighter, then attempted to get on top of me. I fought viciously against him, kicking and yelling at the top of my lungs. I broke his hold on me, somehow forcing him off me. My screaming made him stop and let me go. Had I not escaped he surely would have raped me.

I didn't tell anyone about this. Looking back, I think my parents would have taken me seriously about being grabbed and pulled into that garage.

As an adult and knowing more about life, I realized he was a pedophile. He was a young man married to a beautiful, young woman. They had two infant children. I have often wondered about his children. Were they safe from him? What about the other children in the neighborhood, my playmates... had he done anything to hurt them?

6

❦

Taking a Stand

When I was fifteen, my friends let me know in no uncertain terms, *it was against the law for my dad to hit me the way he did.* "Wow," I said, "Really?" This had not ever occurred to me. I was used to getting hit and not knowing when it would happen.

When I went home that day, I stood up to my dad. I told him, "I found out it is against the law to hit me and, if you hit me again, I will call the police!!"

To say he was shocked, stunned, and angry was an understatement! My mother was standing nearby. My dad turned his back to me. I saw (what looked like to me) steam rising up from him and his head.

Years later, I realized it was an energy I witnessed being released from his crown chakra. He did not hit me ever again. He was different after that confrontation. I've often wondered if this was when that entity/being left my dad and went into me.

I remember looking for birthday and Father's Day cards growing up. It was an emotional job. I found myself putting one after another back into the card rack, feeling resentful, confused, and angry, and also, with a heart filled with love, all simultaneously. I often picked more than one card, ranging in different messages, trying to convey what I felt. Humor was always safe and easily handled. It was the heartfelt ones that were challenging.

I had a very serious talk with my dad in my early forties. I asked him about many things I had questions about. He gave me answers to things I had not understood at an earlier age, finally making sense. It was a good discussion. I asked him demandingly, "Why did you hit me like that, Dad?"

He was sitting in a chair and just hung his head down. He did not look up when he answered, "I don't know. I don't know."

What I saw was an old man sitting there, with his head hung down. I saw an old man who did not have any answers for me. I saw his humbleness. I felt his remorse and sadness. I felt a deep compassion. Understanding came over me. I saw his humanness. I forgave him.

All I could feel from that day forward was forgiveness and my love for all the wonderful things my dad did. The mixed feelings I had about him began to dissipate over time. It was years later that an even deeper, more profound, and complete healing called to be. My inner child had a lot more to say about it.

This is why it is difficult to go back to those past feelings and experiences necessary for this book. Another question may be, what of my younger sister? She says she has no memory of Dad hitting me. Perhaps it's blocked from her memory. My sister simply had a different father experience than I did. Her dad had all of the same wonderful qualities my dad had. The contrast was her father did not hit her. For reasons I would not discover until years later, I was the one he hit.

It took me a long time to realize, this book is not about my sister's opinion or recollection. It is not about anyone other than me and what I felt and what those feelings did to both hinder and enrich my life. What I was given was the biggest gift of all, the opportunity to learn forgiveness and to become empowered because of it. I understand many, many people have had much worse experiences than what I share in this book. My wish for them is that they are blessed with exchanging their suffering for peace and healing.

My sister, her husband, and I took care of our dad during the last two years of his life. When our dad was terminally ill, I was his main caregiver. We were able to care for him at home. I had the opportunity to spend precious time with my dad, twenty-four-seven.

During the last year, my sister's son came to help. It was a privilege and an honor to give back to our dad some of what he had given to us. A tremendous amount of healing took place for me during this irreplaceable time.

7

The End of Innocence

The day after my nineteenth birthday, I came very close to being murdered by a serial rapist. Forty-five years later, I would understand the gift and the blessing from all of this... forty-five years later!

I was abducted, beaten, choked, and raped multiple times before I was able to escape. The man tossed me around as I struggled to fight him off. He threw me down and sat on top of me, pressing his weight on my lungs and on top of my arms, choking me until I began to lose consciousness.

I was a virgin. I was a virgin until that moment. I think of how I proudly held onto my virginity for the right one. To have it forcefully ripped from me bothered me for a very long time. The memory itself haunted and smothered me for what felt like an eternity. Rape is a terrifying, violent experience.

I ended up in the emergency room, and the police were called in. A report was taken, filled with pictures of my bruised body and torn, stained clothing. The attending physician was not consoling or compassionate during the examination. I overheard that doctor snickering to a nurse and making jokes in the next room. Quips such as: "Doesn't her parents have anything better to do than to have her examined?"

I was brutally demeaned. It was excruciating to lie there waiting to be examined and undergo the exam with that doctor. I thought about leaving, running out of there, getting far away. I kept asking myself, "What the hell had happened to me, and why did this happen?!"

It took many years for the scar I had on my leg, from one of the injuries, to finally fade away.

I heard my dad on the phone later. He had called our family doctor seeking help and advice. I was told the doctor assured my dad that he would have it aborted if I were pregnant. I thought, "Do I have anything to say about this?" I felt confused. I felt comforted and at the same time undermined having been left out of any decision-making. Fortunately, I was not pregnant.

The next day, my father and my uncle went out to look for the attacker in the area I had described. They took chains and tire irons with them. I am sure they would have beaten him to death had they found him.

The police found the assailant first and arrested him. My mother begged me to take him to court. It turned out that the rapist was considered a 'big man on campus' at his college and a popular football player. I learned he had a lovely girlfriend who was stunned at his arrest. My attorney informed me that he had a record and had been sentenced to juvenile camp for attempted rape when he was thirteen. Someone came home just as he was about to rape a very young girl. He had also attacked and raped other young women, only they were too humiliated and afraid of him to report it. After his arrest, when the news of his trial spread, some of those women came forward to testify against him and on my behalf. He had also threatened them after he raped them. They didn't need to keep it secret or be afraid anymore.

He was not remorseful. He smirked in court and glared at me. I can't begin to describe how uncomfortable and sinister it felt. I refused to let any of my family into the courtroom during the trial. I could not bear having them hear the details of the attack. It was awful enough to relive it all and explain so many things in a detailed account to a courtroom full of people.

A semen sample had been taken during the examination, and my stained clothes were held up as evidence. I was humiliated and embarrassed. When a person is attacked and raped, it does not just happen to them. It impacts their family and their friends. It can also affect who they date or marry.

Before his trial, while he was out on bail, he spotted me in a store and locked his eyes on mine with unsettling intent. He began following me, uttering disjointed words loudly. I rushed outside through the first door in sight, my heart pounding. He trailed me, his shadow menacing my presence, in body and mind. He bore down on me with intense ranting, mocking, and threats. I bolted toward strangers on the sidewalk. He stopped at that point, yelling, "I'll see you in court!" How did he know where I was that day?

He was found guilty by a jury and sent to prison.

After his release, two or three years later, I was in a dance club with my friends. As I left the ladies' room, all of a sudden, he was there! He grabbed me by my arm, held on tightly, and laughed. He screamed to the people around him, "This is the girl who said I raped her, and I went to prison because of her!" I struggled and broke away from his grip. I quickly returned to where my group of friends were sitting.

Why was he there, and how did he see me?

I did not tell anyone what happened. I was in shock. I did not know how to process what had just happened and all the emotions I felt. I started to cry and asked my friends if we could leave. They did not understand why I was upset. We simply left and went somewhere else.

I have thought back to that event, wondering how different it would have been had I been able to talk and tell my friends what had happened. I am sure it was a violation of his probation to grab and harass me. I am also sure our guy friends would have beaten him, then gone to jail for assault and battery, or worse.

The next day, I told a close friend about running into him. She learned what had happened a few years before. She told her fiancé about it. He later assured me that if I were to see that man again to call him immediately. He and his friends would find my attacker, and I was to let them know "how badly I wanted him beaten and how long I wanted him to be in the hospital."

It did comfort me to know how much my friends cared about my safety and well-being. I really just wanted it all to go away. I wanted to be free of everything that experience represented. I did not wish to resolve it with violence.

Prison did not appear to help his illness, bring any remorse, or soften his heart. However, for me, forgiveness is how I became free. It took years to understand what transpired and how to go about healing and forgiving.

I recall thinking, "I can be free of this. He may be stuck being whatever he is; however, I can be free of this." The realization came to me that I was not the victim. He was the victim. He was stuck being who and what he was. I was free to choose something else for myself. The Ancient Ones again were whispering to me, guiding me in forgiveness and into healing.

I was guided to imagine him standing in front of me, being truly sorry and wanting to make amends. I imagined that I saw how he healed from his dark sickness. It brought me incredible peace to see this in my imagination and to feel in my heart that he found healing.

How much worse is it to be the one inflicting this violence and hatred of self onto another?! However awful it was for me, I knew it was far worse being him, deep in his deranged illness. Imagining his remorse, his heartfelt regret, and his own healing helped me.

A few months after, I was out with a group of friends. We were in a pizza place. It also had a larger room with games and pool tables. On the other side of that room divided by a wall, was a DJ playing dance music with smaller tables to sit at. I sensed someone staring at me. I looked around and recognized him, the aggressor, standing across the room watching me, throwing eye-daggers through me.

It was startling to see him again. But this time, I was different. I immediately went over to security. I told them the man had been sent to prison for raping me and had grabbed my arm and harassed me after he was released. They assured me they would secure him and have the police pick him up if he made any move towards me. He saw me speaking to security and left before anyone could go over to him. That was the last time I saw anything of him.

It eventually dawned on me that he had been stalking me, before and after his trial and imprisonment.

Approximately forty-five years later, when I was sixty-five years old, I had an Ah-ha moment (whispers from the Ancient Ones) about the serial rapist. It was revealed to me that this was a soul agreement, and I was to offer healing for him. I contacted Margaret McCormick, whom my friend, Kyle, recommended for entity removals. I paid to have the entities removed from him. Margaret later informed me there was a very dark one in his brain and an even darker one in his sex organs. She was shown that those came into him around the age of twelve. She also told me she hadn't seen anything quite like that in over thirty years of entity removal.

The gift and blessing for me was to offer him release from the entities driving him. At least on my end, I felt complete closure. I received the gift and the blessing from that experience.

Sometimes, things do not make sense to me still. I often feel I certainly could have found a greater gift in avoiding that entire experience. Life happens for us, even when it does not appear to be so. We only perceive a small amount of all there is going on around us. This leaves most of what there is to know and see, unknown and unseen.

I am developing my ability to be aware of more, to see the unseen, and to rise above the distractions of the five senses in this journey here in the holographic, seemingly physical world. In this simulation and projected reality.

**It is for the brave who wish to take their heads
out from the sand and to know more.**

8

⟨⟩⧼⧽

Hawaii

Soon after, I moved to Maui, Hawaii, for a few years during the early 1970s. It was a wonderful place of beauty and discovery. There was only one condominium in Kihei back then. The road to Makenna Beach was a narrow, unpaved, dirt road. There were Keave trees (with thorns) along the pathway from the road to the beach. Makena was a sweet and peaceful black sand beach. It seemed to be a sacred area. There were no buildings anywhere. Lahaina was a quiet town of restaurants and shops with a harbor. The Maui Sheraton Hotel in Lahaina had only been open for a short time. The west side of Maui was untouched. There were no buildings and only a few dwellings.

It was a glorious adventure of camping, walking along exquisite beaches, and simple lifestyles. Looking back, it was more of a relatively undiscovered, third-world country of simplicity, just beginning to blossom into something unrecognizable today.

Little did I know, it was a land of wilderness, freedom, and danger. As I lived there, along with the fun beach life, collecting shells, creating art, and working in the cafes and restaurants, I began to recognize that almost every woman I met or knew had been beaten and/or raped, either by a stranger, her boyfriend, or her husband!

It was not uncommon for a woman to be in an abusive relationship. What the hell was going on here? I was really opening my eyes to a silent world of accepted abuse and violence.

I remember one of my friends getting hit in front of me by her fiancé. He saw us walking on the way to town from the beach. He stopped his car and got out, yelling at her, then started hitting her. He was extremely drunk. He took another swing at her. I pulled her out of the way, and instead, I was hit in the face. I fell to the ground, shocked! He suddenly stopped, stunned and delirious. She helped me up. We ran and got away from him.

She stayed with another friend that evening and went home the next day. The next day, he was sober and regretful. He talked her into coming back home, pulling her back into his world with false promises. Things were okay for a while until the next time. His following outburst and attack was vicious. My friend was beaten black and blue.

There was a storage room upstairs, above the restaurant I worked in. No one other than the restaurant staff knew about it. I got permission from the owner to hide my friend there until we could sneak her off to the airport. Two days later, she got on a flight and went home to New York. It was a terrifying, painfully sad time for her. She did not go back with him. She did not return to Hawaii. She was fortunate to have a family to go home to and restart her life.

9

The Unexpected

One evening, my boyfriend of over a year came home after drinking and partying with friends. Jr had been a very attentive and
kind boyfriend up until this evening. But on this night, out of
nowhere, Jr Jerk Face began screaming obscenities at me and behaving
insanely. (What?!) It was as if he had lost his mind. I was unable to
reason with him. It only made it worse. I tried to get out of the house
but couldn't get out the door; he blocked me. I tried a window. He
grabbed me and hit me several times.

I fought back but was no match for his crazed rage. Jr tore apart
the house, breaking things, ripping clothes out of the closet, and tear-
ing them up. He dragged me by my hair to his car as I screamed for
help. He managed to shove me into his car, still hanging onto me by
my hair. He yelled, "I am taking you out to the cane fields to kill you!"
I did not doubt this. His eyes were gone. There was a flashing red, di-
abolical presence glaring out where his brown eyes normally were.

I tried grabbing the car keys from the ignition, but he punched me
in the face. He drove us into the night out towards miles of open land,
where the cane and pineapple fields began. I watched as we sped past
the last few houses in the area.

Suddenly, towering cane stalks swayed ahead, bowing violently as
if whispering a warning to go no further. "You'll never make it back,"

they said. Seeing a dim, flickering house light as a final beacon of safety, I flung my door open and jumped out of the car. I bolted to the residence with screams so chilling that I seemed to shatter the night air. Jr's car skidded to a stop. House lights popped on. I heard Jr lurch from his car. I couldn't run fast enough; he closed in from behind.

A porch light blinked awake, illuminating a woman and her husband opening their front door. I lunged forward, my heart stopping, and a beat later, I felt Jr retreating. Without a word, he got into his car and raced off.

Those angels took me in. They saved my life that night. My hair was ripped out of my scalp in some places. I had two black eyes, a bruised face, broken ribs, torn clothes, a broken heart, and a very confused mind. Two days later, when Jr Jerk Face found out where I was, he apologized and tried to convince me to give him another chance. He told me he had smoked pot laced with something, combined with a lot of alcohol.

This was the cycle of abuse: violence, remorse, promises, and violence again. Many were caught in this conditioned, seemingly accepted way of life. Or, these women were too afraid and silenced to successfully get away.

I drank when I was out with my friends. However, I did not use drugs or smoke anything. I learned more from Jr's family about his history of hitting his other girlfriends and beating them. He had a pattern of violence. His father was violent earlier in his marriage. The cycle continued through him. The violence just happened later with me, rather than earlier in our relationship.

The woman who helped me that night had a long talk with me about domestic abuse and alcoholism. She was happily married; however, she shared all she went through with her former fiancé. He was an alcoholic whom she had loved very much. She spoke frankly and with blunt honesty about his desire to change, but was unable to.

I knew I had to leave. I also knew I needed to play it smart. (Whispers from the Ancient Ones). I told Jr I was going to work. He went off somewhere, thinking he'd see me later. I went to work and let them know I needed to get off the island that same day. They gave me my wages in cash. I called the police for help.

The police said they would meet me at my house, and they could only wait outside my home while I packed my clothes. It was not within their authority to do anything else. One of my friends drove me to the airport. I got on a flight to Oahu with my dog and left Maui.

I was one of the fortunate ones. I was able to leave him. At that time in Hawaii, on Maui, there were no domestic violence laws to protect women from being beaten, whether they were married, living with a man, or dating them. The best the police did was to stand outside your home while you packed your things to leave. Or, if they were witnessing an attack in action, they could break it up.

I moved in with friends. An extra room was waiting for me. Several months later, my sister followed me. But it wasn't only her. Jr trailed me. He went to therapy, although he continued to drink. And, he love-bombed me by buying me Raisins the bunny rabbit for a pet. Emotional numbness and fears of retaliation had a hold of me. I kept my focus on helping my sister leave her abusive relationship with Sneaky Snake. I was also busy working while I pursued modeling.

We had several run-ins with Sneaky Snake. For the final encounter, he came to my house, and I saw him from my window. I ran to meet him outside and stood boldly at the top of the stairs. He approached me, but I wouldn't budge. I stood there in front of him and fiercely declared: "If you take one more step up here, I will knock you down these stairs and beat the shit out of you!" I glared into his eyes defiantly, and he backed off. I was aggressively protecting my sister.

That night, I helped my sister pack and drove her to the airport the next day. She got on a flight home to the mainland. As I was driving away from the airport, I saw her ex-boyfriend walking around looking for her. "Too bad, she's safe from you now," I thought.

A few months after my sister left, I moved to a shared house near Waikiki. I was doing well with modeling. It was inspiring, challenging, and fun. One of the coordinators, a happily married, very successful model, shared about a former boyfriend who would not leave her alone. I've always wondered if she saw something in me. Jr had not been to the agency located in the Royal Hawaiian Hotel. (At least, not that I knew of). I did see him at times, and he was often around.

A year and a half later, I finally answered the call to return to the mainland to my family. "It's time for you to leave Hawaii. It's time for you to return home," I kept hearing. (Whispers from the Ancient Ones aka Spirit). I left the land of Hawaii I loved so very much. I was forced to leave the place dear to my heart, not realizing that the dark shadow would pursue me all the way to the mainland.

Before leaving Oahu, several of us were chosen to go to the Philippines. Three men from an agency were selecting models for a huge promotional event. I was not chosen for the final round. They'd decided on a smaller group of models. I'd felt disappointed. Two weeks later, I overheard the owner and the manager talking. "No one has heard back from them." I still didn't know what happened when I left. I've often thought of them. Were they okay? I realized I'd been protected.

On the mainland, Jr found me at home and pretended to be someone he was not around my family. Although I never told Dad that Jr ever beat me, he apparently figured it out. That night I told Dad, "I don't want to go with Jr anymore." The next morning, my father drove Jr to the airport, bought him a one-way ticket to Maui, and watched Jr board and fly away.

When dad returned in the afternoon, I asked him, "What happened?"

Dad replied, "I told him you didn't want to be with him." This is all he would ever say about it.

I thought I would return to Hawaii after spending time with my family. I'd left my dog and my rabbit with friends. Back then, it was quite an ordeal to take your animals to Hawaii. There was a two-week quarantine required to bring in a pet. I didn't want to put them through this.

Later, I was told my dog died of a broken heart, and my rabbit also died. This felt worse than all I'd been through. I spent years consoling my inner child and forgiving myself for that situation. It feels as though she has finally recovered. I've seen my dog and rabbit come back to me in other fur kids. It's been resolved.

10

My Beloved Mother

Just before Christmas of 1986 when I was thirty-six, my beloved mother unexpectedly died. She was sixty-six, much too young to leave us. To say I was not prepared was beyond an understatement. Her death sent me into a tailspin of loss. I was inconsolable. I had no idea how to even begin to deal with the bottomless, endless abyss of pain I felt. I felt a part of me went with her.

At the hospital, I had my arms around my mother, lying across her body, sobbing, just knowing if I stayed there, she would come back into her lifeless body. I could feel her spirit right there, so close! My family gently pulled me away twice. Everyone was crying, grieving, shocked, and numb.

I recalled reading about men who often die within a year of their wife's passing. As I drove away from the hospital with my father, I turned to him and said," I hope you do not plan on going anywhere anytime soon! We need you here. Andrew (my nephew) needs you!" My dad just looked at me. It went in. He got it. He understood what I was saying. My dad lived another twenty years. He was there for his family. He chose not to remarry. He did not date and seemed to be content with his family and friendships. He had enjoyed a forty-year marriage to the love of his life.

I functioned reasonably well until the next day. At our family home, I sat at my mother's vanity, my heart longing for one more moment, one more word from the woman whose love filled this space just days prior. I put on some of my mother's jewelry and just sat there silently, looking in the mirror, desperately wanting to feel a connection with my mom. I needed her next to me somehow. Wearing Mom's jewelry felt like a way to feel a part of her and to have her still with me. My sister came in and saw me with the jewelry on. She blurted out, "I gave that to Mom! Why are you wearing it?!" My sister had no idea what I was feeling, or what my intention was, and she was deep in her own grief.

This was all it took for me to go over the edge. Something broke inside of me. After that moment, I wasn't the same. I ran from the house and drove to someone who could help me- to a connection who could get me what I thought I needed. I turned to drugs and drinking to keep myself numb. I was unable to help with anything after that. I couldn't bring myself to go to our family home. I couldn't get myself to help my sister choose our mother's funeral dress. I did not help with anything after that.

I missed my mother's funeral.

In my apartment bedroom, I completely flipped out. I snapped, lost control, gave way to the pain and anger. I threw things against the wall, breaking glasses, picture frames, and porcelain figures, screaming at God and my mother, "Fuck you, God!! Why did my mom have to die?!" I wailed, "Fuck you, Mom! How could you die and leave me?!"

I was distraught, overcome with grief, and in immeasurable pain. The other excruciatingly raw wounds and memories resurfaced, rising from a concealed place deep within me. Everything demanded attention all at the same time. The torrent of anger, fear, and hate whirling inside, rising like a tornado, and the wave of grief and despair crashing over me, drowned me in a dark sea. It was beyond overwhelming.

My worried family did not know what had happened when I did not show up at the funeral. My sister and cousin, Patty, came to my apartment. They knocked on my door for ages, very worried. I couldn't bring myself to answer the door. My sister was on her way to the manager to ask for help getting into my apartment. Patty called me on the phone, and for some reason, I answered. She said, "I know your heart has been ripped out. Please open the door so I can come in, Cuz." (Our nickname for each other was Cuz.)

Something in her heartfelt plea reached me. I opened the door. They came in and saw the emotional mess I was in. While dealing with their own grief and pain, they reached out to help me. It was decided that I would move back to our family home. It felt right. It helped me to feel I could be there for my dad when I wasn't at work. My sister also moved back to our family home. We were there for quite a while, each healing in our own way and helping each other heal simply by being there together.

A couple of weeks later, an older friend- the one who supplied me with cocaine and valium- said to me, "I know your mommy died, but you can't bury yourself, too." Something in the way he said this caused a shift in me.

Those words made it into my inner being and allowed me to open up and listen. I was able to stop my numbing methods and soothe myself. I began to gather the strength to step into grieving and begin a healing process.

I do not recommend drugs to anyone. I didn't make a wise choice. I was very fortunate to have made it out of that wrong choice, quickly. I know I had the grace of God and benevolent beings shoring me up, guiding me, and supporting me when I was lost.

I had undergone what is referred to as a "functional breakdown." I was able to carry on while feeling broken and emotionally shredded. It seemed as though a connection in my mind had gotten unplugged, disconnected. I had been excellent in spelling before this. I found myself needing to relearn spelling. It took me quite a while to get my spunk back. It was five years before I could hear a song my mother had sung without tears running down my face.

I had a lot of forgiving to do. I had deep, confusing pain to heal. I had to forgive myself for screaming at God and blaming my mother, the embarrassment of turning to drugs and drinking, falling apart and breaking down, letting my family down, and letting myself down. There was so much to face, forgive, and to heal from.

Years later, these same experiences provided the wisdom to help others heal. I was brought in as an expert for clinical hypnotherapy, nutrition, and healing work for private, substance-abuse recovery homes. I understood some of the pain, confusion, guilt, etc., many of these brave souls felt. I saw entities in several of them and I had also learned how to remove them.

In 1987, I found myself writing as though someone was pouring wisdom, guidance, and inspiration through me. I wondered if it was my mother guiding me from beyond... Whispers from the Ancient Ones...

It was then that I wrote and self-published, "Our Guide To Life Is The Voice Within, The Insight Into Our Insight." It included what I had learned about forgiveness back then and other spiritual under-standings I knew at the time. This book is, in a way, an extension of my first writings. It is key to remember, forgiveness also includes self-forgiveness. This can be the most difficult element of forgiving: resolving the guilt, inner beliefs, judgments- the programmed messages we receive in this world.

Forgiveness is similar to mourning and healing grief, it usually happens in stages.

**As we remember to comfort the inner child, hear the inner child,
and bring new understanding to the inner child,
it becomes much easier to forgive ourselves
for perceived mistakes and perceived failures.**

Part Two: Wounds to Wisdom

The Ultimate Tools for Transforming Through Forgiveness
Discover the powerful tools and transformative insights you need to release pain, reclaim your strength, and find true inner freedom. This is your guide to letting go, healing deeply, and stepping into a life empowered by grace and compassion.

11

The Beginning of Healing

I have had my share of dating and serious relationships. I didn't always select the "cream of the crop" in men, and even some of my friends. I seemed to feel comfortable with someone who needed help or "fixing."

When I did find myself with a good quality man, I was not ready for it, even though I certainly wanted to be ready. I was trying to fix myself through other people. I was reaching out to heal the pain I had deep within myself. I later learned this was trauma bonding.

When I was fifty-six, I wondered if I was trapped in some weird dimension or time warp. A life in time where I saw other people happily together; however, it would never happen for me. Nevertheless, my inner knowing knew I had a soul mate life partner. (Whispers from the Ancient Ones). I knew we would meet and continue our lives together. Why was it taking so long?!

After many years of working on healing the anger, pain, and confusion, working with forgiveness, learning different modalities of healing and transformation, and even more healing... my 'perfect for me husband' came into my life. It took the time needed for us to be ready for each other.

Soulmates and life partners come together when the timing is right for both people.

I am seventy-four now and happily married to my best friend. We met later in life when I was fifty-nine. He was fifty-eight. Does this make me a Cougar? I'll let you decide while I smile mischievously.

It is not necessary to be perfect or to find the perfect person. It is only necessary to be working on our own stuff, practicing forgiveness, and healing within to be really ready to take on the even deeper work. This deeper work and healing often comes along when the 'perfect for you person' comes into your life.

My husband and I have a loving relationship and a wonderful life together. We work together on our relationship to keep it healthy and maintained. Marriage is a commitment we commit to each day. There have been times of frustration, arguments, anger, and misunderstanding which we worked through.

When our person does show up and we come together, any inner wounds (our stuff) will come up and surface. It usually pops up unpredictably and in surprising ways. It may not be easy. It requires patience, tenacity, commitment, and a willingness to go through it. Forgiveness is the power tool to get us through it all, to transmute discord, and to be who and what we really are- instruments of peace.

Forgiveness will dissipate the everyday frustrations and the annoyances we may have with other people in our lives and with ourselves. The ego does not want peace or forgiveness. It likes to hold onto things and chew on them. It wants to keep the hot rock burning. The heart and mind, however, require peace.

Forgiveness can also help us deal with disappointments and expectations. Ah, yes, our expectations. As we become aware of our preconceived expectations and release them, we become even freer.

12

Learning More About Forgiveness

There are many ideas, philosophies, beliefs, and theories about God and what the reality of our existence really is. Of the many things in life, I am not certain about, I do know without any doubt, these things:

1. When we get out of our own way, let go, and allow-
   miracles can then take place.

2. Forgiveness equals peace, every time.
   Every time I practice forgiveness, I always receive peace.

3. Our thoughts can become physical things.
   What we think is powerful. It creates our world for us. Our thoughts lead us to our emotions.

4. Forgiveness is essential to healing.
   It all begins with this action of absolution, of absolving all fault or blame.

Forgiveness is always about me when I am forgiving, and it is always about our individual self when we choose to forgive. It is not about any other person, place, or thing.

Others may benefit from our forgiveness; however, it is not about anyone or anything else outside of ourselves. When we forgive others, we are rescuing places within ourselves that were wounded and plead to be comforted and made whole again. When we begin to heal, we shift and change. Our outside world "cannot, not change" as our inner world transforms.

Forgiveness and compassion are the way out of pain, suffering, disappointment, fear, frustration, distress, and unhappiness of any kind. It is this simple.

It begins and ends with us. It begins and ends with me.

Prana manna moma a   light body of bliss, Male

It is not always easy to do. It can take a great deal of practicing forgiveness to get into the habit of forgiving. We may not want to even begin to think about forgiving. Yet it is the key- the necessary thing to do to be reunited with our inner sanctuary.

There have been times I did not know how to forgive something, someone, or myself. There are situations I did not feel the desire to forgive. I realized it even more when I felt resentment.

When I find myself stuck, I call upon a higher power to help me. I offer it up and place it on the altar of the Holy Spirit. Then I let it go, knowing it will be resolved.

Consider God means: Get Own Description. It is a word or words describing a higher power we resonate with.

You Great Spirit who is known by a thousand names yet is the unnamable One. This is an excerpt taken from opening/closing sacred space in shamanic ceremonies.

If someone does not believe in a higher power, they could ask life itself to help. We are alive; therefore, there is energy of life flowing through the air we breathe. We can utilize this to help us with forgiveness.

The point is to ask for help. It doesn't matter what someone else believes in. At times, we may feel lost and disconnected from knowing. Just ask for assistance. It's okay to feel afraid. Courage is acting in spite of fear.

Once I have asked, I feel calm. I sense a flow, a shift of moving from unyielding emotions into forgiveness. I feel peaceful again. Everything shifts, exchanging the distress for my inner sanctuary.

The only real work is to at least "want-to-want to" forgive. It is not necessary to know how.

The desire to forgive brings about the rest of the miracle of peace. It is one of the most empowering experiences we can have.

**Compassion and forgiveness are love in action.
Love is the highest power.**

Forgiveness is not religious or a religion. It is simply how we find our way away from the distractions (pain) and back to the reality of being one with peace. With inner peace, so much more becomes possible... joy, health, love, fun, healing, understanding, prosperity, etc.

It seems we "cannot, not" judge. It becomes necessary to evaluate and determine if it is safe to cross the street, enter into an unknown neighborhood, check to be sure our shoes match, decide if the food we are buying is fresh, and so on. Judgment is a part of living in this world. This type of judgment is discernment. We check to find out if this is right for us. Judgment referred to here regarding forgiveness is condemning someone or something.

Our unconscious mind takes each judgment about others very personally and applies this internally to itself as if it were true for itself. When we judge others and condemn them as bad or wrong, we add to the unconscious guilt we have.

**Whatever we judge and condemn in another,
we are judging and condemning in ourselves.
This is how the unconscious area of the mind works.**

No matter what it may look like through our words and actions, we each seek peace. We each desire harmonious lives. We each want to be accepted. We each want to feel we are whole and complete just as we are. We are led to see something very different in our dualistic world. We may only see the illusion of being something other than one with the omnipresent One.

Regardless, forgiveness simply means we are able to free ourselves from being tied to anger, hatred, resentment, fear, pain, humiliation, distrust, shame, guilt, etc. We receive freedom from the experience. It brings peace and helps heal. It energetically releases us from whomever or whatever we are forgiving. Forgiveness also allows healing for the person or circumstance. I believe we desire, at the deepest part of ourselves, to heal, to be free; and for the offender to heal, also.

Again, when we forgive others, we are really forgiving the places within us that are wounded and need healing. It is not about the other person or situation. It is always about our own self-healing.

Forgiveness is one of the most empowering experiences we can have. It is love in action. Love is the highest power. Peace is a beautiful way to find our way back from the pain and back to the reality of being one with peace. Peace brings infinite possibilities. I believe we each seek peace.

As I learned more about different healing modalities, I healed further, and I healed deeper. The anger, pain, and feelings of not being enough lessened. My life became less dramatic. The quality of my relationships improved. I eventually came to understand that all acts of violence (and judgments that condemn) are acts of self-hatred. By placing the unconscious guilt onto someone or something else, it serves as a temporary reprieve.

Condemnations are subtle acts of violence and self-hatred we can do in small, seemingly insignificant ways each day. We can do this without realizing how consequential our thoughts and actions really are. It can become second nature to us.

In one of my NLP trainings, our instructor, Nicholas, told us, "Imagine that people are always doing the best they can, with where they are in life and what they know at the time." He continued, "no matter what it is they are doing or how they could do things differently if they were only aware and if they knew how."

That was a lot for me to take in and process. Yet, it helped me make sense of some people's horrific actions. To quote Marianne Williamson: "Everything we do is either an act of love or a cry for help."

People scream for help in the ways they act.

Forgiveness has given me my freedom from anything I have ever attempted to blame someone or something else for. It has brought me peace and contentment and a freedom I was always running towards.

It is a continuing process. As we live our lives, we encounter more experiences. We can get our feelings hurt, feel betrayed, become angry, lash out, implode within, etc. We can then create more grievances to heal from. As we practice forgiveness, we are able to go deeper and deeper into the final layers and heal all the way into every cell.

We have over seventy trillion cells in our bodies. Each cell responds to our thoughts, feelings, and experiences. Each cell responds to forgiveness, harmony, and resolution.

Forgiveness is the power tool I used to enable healing within myself. For me, it is the way to Source. It is what I did to move away from pain and heal the traumatic experiences I had in life. In the beginning of wanting to be healed, fear can take a strong hold on directing our path. "What will I be if I do not have my pain and suffering? Who will I be without my stuff that is so much a part of me?"

We can identify with pain and suffering, giving it a life of its own. It is in this that we can become stuck on our path to really being who we are and all we can become in our lives. We can become very attached to our wounds and illnesses. There may be a secondary gain from staying wounded, remaining ill, and keeping our anger or grief. Often this is unknown and thereby more challenging to identify and become aware of. Until someone is really ready to shed this aspect and step outside of what has become second nature to them, there may not be real peace for them.

Remember, we only need to *want to* want to. From there, the process begins, motivated by peace. Peace becomes the priority. Everything we want and need is right there, just outside of our comfort zone.

When I catch myself in judgment of someone else, I use forgiveness to continue healing the unconscious. I stop and ask myself, "What is this reflecting to me I have within myself that I need to heal?" I may not know what it is or how to forgive it. I simply stop and ask, setting the intention to forgive.

Healing is a continuous voyage throughout life. Our choice then becomes: "How much of any discord will I let in, and how long will I allow it to disrupt my life?" This is the power of absolving whatever is in the way of the path to peace. We have empowerment over anything that may come our way.

The vital key to loving others more is to take care of ourselves first in order to take care of others. For example, saying no when needed and having boundaries, even though others may not like it. Being gentle with ourselves, forgiving ourselves, cherishing ourselves, and releasing guilt. These all allow us to love ourselves. We are completely full and taken care of when loving ourselves.

I have sat with nature, the trees, air, clouds, water, and asked for assistance in forgiving. There are times when forgiveness does not flow easily. Or, something shows up later for a deeper release.

Whispers from the Ancient Ones: "Forgive what you can. Do your best. Forgive what you cannot forgive. Forgive what you cannot let go of. Let go of the rest. Life supports you. We support you."

13

Thoughts Are Physical Things

When do we mistake surviving for thriving and mistake upheaval for fate? When we feel unheard and unseen, can we mistake heartache for a test of faith?

A disruptive childhood can lead to events in adulthood mirroring our wounds. Cycles of abandonment, betrayal, or struggle feel more familiar than peace. Ever loyal to what it has known, the body becomes addicted to pain in ways we often don't recognize.

Equating the familiar with safety, the body can mistake suffering for security, chaos for control, and longing for love. Once trained by hardship, the nervous system craves the patterns that seemingly broke us and searches for recognizable feelings, drawing us toward circumstances to repeat what it deems 'normal.'

If we wish to break this pattern, we must interrupt the body's programs, cravings, and habitual reactions. Forgiveness interrupts. It instills the perception of 'everything is all right with the world,' so we can move toward what is right with the world. Forgiveness breaks patterns that draw us into spaces that affirm that 'nothing is right with the world.' In this shadowy space where harmony has unraveled, unrest reigns.

What happens when love is equated to harm and love becomes an addiction- one shaped by the trauma of a three or four-year-old watching one parent strike the other? ... an absent parent, even one leaving to return only to leave again... an abusive parent (or parents)? The addict must get their fix, and the adult child is unconsciously drawn into discordant experiences until that program is replaced with pure love.

The subconscious mind takes things very personally. "This must be true of me," it says. Children do not just observe, they absorb. They become what they witness and experience. Their definition of what love is for them is hard-wired into their nervous system by the age of five. For a child, the world revolves around their caretakers (or lack thereof). Every experience is internalized as a reflection of their worth and how they are loved.

If violence is intertwined with love from an early age, the body learns to crave discord, long for what it knows, even when it is not truly love. As this child grows, their nervous system seeks the familiar- subconsciously recreating the same painful patterns to reaffirm their place at the center of their world, to convince themselves they are still loved, even when love and harm have become inseparable.

The body seeks what it knows. It does not seek happiness.
Forgiveness collapses the program. It retrains the body
to recognize that peace and love are not threats. It creates new
neural pathways in the brain. Forgiveness propels our
bodies beyond suffering into an existence that attracts peace.

The neuroscientist and pharmacologist Candace Pert, Ph.D., made an amazing discovery in the late 1990s. It revealed exactly why we manifest certain relationships, emotional patterns, abundance- or not, and good health- or not. Her groundbreaking research bridged the gap between neuroscience and holistic health- between the mind and emotional well-being. Her work uncovered why we feel the emotions we feel. It also clarified why it can be so challenging to change our behaviors.

While Dr. Pert was a chief in the Brain Biochemistry section of the National Institutes of Health, she discovered:
OUR THOUGHTS ARE REAL, PHYSICAL THINGS.

Our thoughts become molecules the instant we think them, and as deliberate attractors, we need to know how those molecules interact with our bodies. She appeared as the expert in the documentary "What the #$*! Do We Know?" [1]

Every time we have a thought, our hypothalamus, a control center near the base of the brain, transforms this thought into millions of neuropeptides. Those neuropeptides represent the dominant emotion behind the thought. Those molecules, with the weight of emotion, course through the body. Millions transporting glee or doubt, surprise or sorrow. Our thought becomes a molecular messenger of emotion! Then the bloodstream is flooded with those neuropeptides, with the gravity of our feelings. When in our bloodstream, these neuropeptides insert themselves into our cells.

Each neuropeptide interlocks with a special receptacle (made just for it) on our cell's membrane- just as a lock fits into a keyhole. This amino-acid chain is then absorbed by our cells. Dr. Pert found that over time, our cells develop more and more special receptors for the neuropeptides to which they are most exposed. Our cells create a self-fulfilling emotional prophecy. Our cells begin to crave the neuropeptides to which they are most exposed and have built all the receptors for. Then, they direct our hypothalamus to produce what they are craving.

Our cells crave the neuropeptides, our emotions to which they are most exposed, and direct our hypothalamus to produce more of what they are craving!

I wanted more acceptance, safety, and love during and after childhood. You may have wanted more of the same. Regardless, my cells had a different agenda. They craved anxiety, and my compliant brain delivered! "Who needs peace when we can have turmoil?" my cells replied.

Our cells love neuropeptides so much that they cover their membranes only with receptors for them and shut down other vital functions. Our cells become vessels for these neuropeptides, just like a drug addict becomes a basin for narcotics.

The only way our hypothalamus can produce the neuropeptides craved by our cells is for our brain to experience the emotions that will create them. The only way our brain can experience the emotions necessary to create those neuropeptides is for it to create a reality that will produce those emotions. Our body literally becomes physically addicted to certain emotional states. This has nothing to do with whether those emotional states feel good or bad; our cells now NEED them.

What can we do about this? There are many avenues proven to rehabilitate our cells and help transition negative addiction to positive habits and patterns. Forgiveness is a major step toward restoration.

When it's difficult to take a first step, try these four techniques:

1. Send your issue onto the altar of a higher power. Then let go. Leave it there. If your mind returns to the issue, place it back onto the altar. Repeat as needed.

2. If anxiety affects breathing, stand up, walk around, then stop.
Breathe out all the air in your lungs.
Without inhaling, swallow.
Breath out any remaining air.
Swallow, exhale again.
This allows the lungs to relax. Now take in a full breath.

3. Set aside ten minutes each day to meditate with the intention to build the desire to forgive.
During your meditation, notice any areas of discomfort in your body.
Place your hands over the area- this sends healing there.
Repeat daily until any discomfort has eased and you have embodied self-forgiveness.

4. 'Crisscross walking' distracts your mind and resets your system.
Swing your right arm forward while moving your left foot forward.
Swing the left arm forward while moving the right foot forward.
Do this for ten minutes.

The power of forgiveness exchanges peace for pain. It leads us out of emotional cell addiction. This must start with self-forgiveness, or a hole is left for our power to leak out.

Research shows us many things help heal cellular emotional addiction. Examples are meditation, NLP, Hypnotherapy, affirmations, yoga, chanting, sound therapy, music, Reiki, Pranic Healing, exercise, grounding, spending time with nature, as well as counseling or therapy.

I took advantage of all of these, with forgiveness being my main power tool.

[1] *What the #$! Do We Know!?**, directed by William Arntz, Betsy Chasse, and Mark Vicente (Roadside Attractions, 2004), DVD.

14

❧

Timeless Peace

I sometimes think back to Neuro Linguistic Practitioner's (NLP) Master Practitioner's training... what it was like accepting the challenge of breaking a one-inch thick, 12" x 12" wood board with my bare hand. This literal and metaphorical exercise of overcoming barriers was a significant part of the course.

I had eagerly looked forward to it for months, knowing it would be life-changing. However, I had no real information on what I'd be learning... exactly. Mystery surrounded what went on in the training. I knew I'd learn more Hypnosis techniques and gain advanced NLP skills. Master practitioners spoke of huge personal breakthroughs. I was excited to discover what awaited me.

Board-breaking day arrived. I had a quiet knowing within- I would complete this challenge. I went on faith and trust, allowing myself to be led to the how. The 'how' would only be revealed the moment that the moment presented itself.

On the back of our boards, we wrote the things we wanted to break through and be free of. We wrote our fears, limited beliefs, personal challenges, etc. On the front side of our boards, we weaved the story of what we chose to bring into our lives. We were encouraged to decorate our boards however we wanted. The more we added to our boards- the more we narrated greater possibilities and illustrated living who we were to become- the more connected we became with our desired realities and anticipated outcomes.

On the front of my board, I placed the dreams and goals I wanted to see realized- a future free from the weight of my past. I envisioned a version of myself untouched by old wounds, stepping into joy, success, and love. The face of my board, looking like a sunlit beach with dolphins, represented me truly at peace, no longer defined by the memories that once held me captive.

The day before, a board had split in two on its own! This undeniable sign of unseen forces at work had resulted from the student's breakthrough. An instructor explained that the student had just gone through such a transformation that the powerful new reflection of herself was put into motion before her hand reached her board. This amazing energy we carry within us- vast and largely untapped- is the driving force behind profound change, whether annihilating self-deprecating thoughts, collapsing a program that keeps us in fear, or fracturing a piece of wood in front of our faces.

We were shown YouTube videos displaying how the board breaks before the hand actually touches it.

The intention and the buildup of energy from the mind direct this energy to move through the hand. **The hand does not break the board.** The intensity of the energy moving from the hand breaks the board.

I watched and listened as my instructor broke his board first. He explained a few things and left the rest for us to figure out on our own.

Breaking the board was also a lesson and demonstration in "modeling"- doing exactly what someone else does to succeed. He also informed us, "Not everyone breaks their board the first time."

I thought, "The worst that can happen is I injure my hand and not break the board." As my thoughts continued to process, I told myself, "I can take this chance, because I just might actually be able to do this amazing feat- me! Other people have done this before me. If they can do it, I can do it. I know I can."

I decided to trust and have faith. I let it all go. I observed, listened, and absorbed everything I could as the others went up, set up their boards, took position, gathered their energy, and directed their intentions. Each student went through a few mock hits and proceeded to break their board! With unwavering focus, each person broke the thick, solid-wood board on their first attempt.

Unwavering focus unlocks transformative powers within us, shattering the barriers of our past. However, if our bodies remain fixated on trauma, painful patterns are reinforced. Focused intention frees us from emotional weight, allowing our hidden energies to surge forward, turning even the most challenging situations into opportunities for profound change.

It was my turn. I walked up to my spot and took my position. I let go of any doubts. I dismissed the possibility of injuring myself. I became very still and centered. My mind was tranquil. I was quiet inside... surprisingly. I allowed myself to become tremendously focused. I opened a place within myself to allow, really allow. I tested my move a few times. I took a step back and drew the energy from my mind, down into my arm, and through my hand. I flew my hand down directly upon the board and WHAM!! I broke my board!

The split second I entered the zone of my energy hitting the board, I was swept into the realm of eternal continuity. I was literally connected to everything, and at the same moment, nothingness. It was extraordinary, unexplainable peace beyond peace; stillness; be-ing, without be-ing. An instant without time or existence. I was in the void! I was in the field of unlimited, pure potentiality where everything is whole and healed. There was no sound, no motion, no feeling, and no thought. It just was.

This did something within me. I became aware of the amazing consciousness of what can be accomplished by allowing, trusting, and following through. Knowing without knowing.

Whispers from the Ancient Ones: "Here's something for you."

Timelessness. I was swept into an unchanging essence, into a realm of perpetual continuity, where our inner power is everlasting and cannot fade.

When you want to bring something into the state of 'already healed' utilize the following exercise, which is an example of needing money to pay a substantial bill:

1. Claim and affirm: "Prosperity is a continuous, unchanging state and any perceptions of lack are already healed."
2. Stand in a place in nature representing a power spot to you.
3. Set up your imaginary board.
4. Position your body in a power stance.
5. Maintain this position as your body embraces its truth- 'it is a sacred urn holding your power.'
6. Release doubts.
7. Dismiss fears.
8. Connect to inner quiet and stillness.
9. Draw energy in through your crown chakra, allowing it to flow into your body. Direct this energy into your shoulder, down your arm, and into your hand.
10. Now break your board! ... breaking any beliefs of lack or 'can't be healed' thoughts. You're in the field of pure potentiality!
11. Step into knowing. FEEL IT!
12. Affirm the bill has been paid. The timeless truth rushes in- 'it shall be done.'
13. Allow life to recalibrate to 'you already have it.'
14. Persist in 'knowing you have it.'

Whenever I bring myself back to the state of awareness when I broke my board, I remind myself of 'not needing to know' how miracles manifest in life. I also use this memory when I feel anxious, recalling the amazing peace beyond peace.

We only need to allow ourselves to take command of the unlimited energy that naturally resides and flows within us... all of what we can accomplish, become, and do when utilizing this life force by directing it with our intent. We can accomplish the seemingly impossible.

It is possible to forgive and exchange pain and suffering for peace. I continue to do this. Forgiveness equals peace. Every time. My soul recognizes the spirit of peace and God within you and within all and everything. Nothing else exists outside of ourselves. It's all in the mind. By letting go of the mind's limiting thoughts, the floodgates open and peace rushes in.

Everything we need to have is already present within us.

We are mirror images of one another in terms of our actions, thoughts, needs, and desires. These correlate with the stage of growth or development we are in at the time. It reflects our likes, dislikes, insecurities, and what we feel confident in- where we feel safe and secure. What we dislike about another is an issue within ourselves. When we see this and become aware of it, we can come to terms with it. We heal it within ourselves. We release old patterns, which no longer work. We change beliefs no longer true for us.

Another's reaction to us is not necessarily directed towards us, although it certainly can seem this way. An extraordinary freedom results in taking nothing personally.

People often treat others in the way they feel about themselves. Their inner personal connection with themselves extends to others. If their cells are addicted to chaos, self-hate, or despair, you just might see their mind-body connection in action, trying to get you to be the source of their chaos.

Yet, they may have an attribute that causes you to focus on an inner insecurity- one they also have within themselves. Sometimes another person has a better perception of us than we do. They may see attributes and qualities in us that we are not aware of or concerned with. Listening with an open mind precludes forgiveness, allowing nothingness to rush in where a wound once bled through.

We can make the necessary changes after allowing a new awareness and understanding to take place.
This happens through our own accountability. Each of us knows what changes we would benefit from making to become happier, more loving, and more accepting.
Changes for ourselves and as an active participant in life.

15

Ho'oponopono

HO'OPONOPONO essentially means to make it right with the people with whom we have relationships. It is an ancient Hawaiian practice of reconciliation and forgiveness. I first heard about it in 2008 from my NLP trainer, Nicholas Rave. He told our class about the book *Zero Limits*[2], and its story of profound changes in a psychiatric ward due to the Ho'oponopono.

Authored by Joe Vitale from *The Secret*[3], *Zero Limits* is Joe's journey with Ihaleakala Hew Len, PhD, who created nothing less than miraculous results in healing the violent, mentally ill, and criminal patients in the forensic ward of a Hawaiian state hospital.

The prisoners in this state facility had committed the most vicious crimes of rape, murder, and violence. They were taken there for evaluation to see if they were capable of standing trial for their crimes. Violent outbreaks were frequent and relentless. Fearing for their lives, the staff endured attacks, injuries, and constant threats.

Patients were heavily medicated to keep them controllable. Many were in restraints, kept in padded cells, held in isolation rooms, or bound by other desperate means. One nurse's account described the atmosphere as so dismal that paint peeled off the walls. Staff members called in sick regularly. Personnel walked closely to walls opposite the constrained patients. There was no self-care. Patients were never taken outside, and visitors were rare.

Over a few months, this forensic ward transformed into a truly astounding environment. Patients began requiring less and less medication. Other than new arrivals, the violent outbursts stopped. Some patients became well enough to be transferred to less stringent facilities. Eventually, patients no longer required restraints. This high-security ward went from understaffed, stressful, and shocking conditions to a happy, wholesome care unit. Some of the patients were allowed outside with staff members. There were cookie-baking activities, and they even held an outdoor car wash. Visitors came to see the patients.

This all occurred because of Dr. Hew Len's work of Ho'oponopono-healing through forgiveness. Remarkably, Dr. Len did not see the patients one-on-one in an office; he did not interact with them, which he normally did with therapy. Instead, he sat in his office with a patient's chart. He meditated on the chart information, on what was written about the crimes and the mentally deranged patient.

Dr. Len asked himself what was being reflected to him about this very ill patient. What about that patient pointed to himself? What did he need to heal within himself?

Dr. Len spent his entire time cleansing and healing himself inwardly while in his office. As he continued day after day, week after week, the patients began to heal and recover. What he healed inwardly showed up as results outwardly in everyone else!

We think of the conscious mind as big and controlling because it is our mental will, thoughts, feelings, and memories. However...

Unseen forces- shaped by past experiences, emotions, and deep-seated beliefs- govern our lives. When they are chaotic, they manifest as disorder. Yet, when cultivated through forgiveness, grace, and alignment with higher energies, they become a source of healing.

Imagine the conscious mind as the size of the room you are sitting in now. This seems very large and powerful, doesn't it? Well, in comparison, the unconscious mind is about the size of the United States. The unconscious is the controlling part of the mind. The conscious, thinking area of the mind is not.

It is estimated that the unconscious makes up ninety to ninety-nine percent of the mind. Our conscious mind is approximately one to five percent of our entire mind. We are not aware of most of the mind. Almost everything we know, everything we have ever learned, heard, or been exposed to, is stored within the unconscious areas of our mind. Who we are, our address, phone number, how to drive, everything comes from the unconscious and is fed down into the conscious part of our mind.

The unconscious mind operates with the innocence and simplicity of a five to seven-year-old, perceiving the world in a raw, unfiltered way. It internalizes external judgments and emotional states like a young child taking on and mimicking the states of people in their environment. Age seven is considered the age of reasoning, where logic begins to shape perception. This insight sheds light on the whys of how things get decided. The unconscious mind forms beliefs and makes decisions based on its inner workings that are deeply ingrained, childlike interpretations formed early in life.

When we judge others, the unconscious mind internalizes those judgments, interpreting them as truths about itself. "If this is true about them, it must be true about me." Just as children absorb and personalize the energies and experiences around them, our unconscious mind takes on the weight of external opinions and events, shaping our inner reality. Therefore, when we judge others, we take on the weight of that judgment. Forgiving others releases that weight.

When we sleep, our conscious mind shuts off. So, what keeps our body breathing? The unconscious mind does. It runs all of our body's systems and brain chemistry and governs whether or not we feel pain, become ill, or heal. It maintains and controls endless processes and activities.

We can feel a change as we allow ourselves to let go of the burden of a negative experience. It takes a tremendous amount of our energy and effort to hold on to heavy emotions. As we release these things, we might find we have more energy and focus to direct toward goals. Our work might improve. We will probably notice we feel happier and more relaxed in general.

The conscious mind is connected to the unconscious mind, and the unconscious is connected to the super-consciousness. The super-conscious mind holds a more expansive and enlightened awareness, beyond the ego and limitations of ordinary consciousness. It gives us perceptions that release neuropeptides carrying optimistic emotions that build happy life experiences, as spoken of in Chapter Thirteen.

How do we tap the super-consciousness? Through forgiveness. Forgiveness creates a funnel from the super-conscious, through the unconscious layers, and finally into our consciousness. Once the conscious mind is open to these higher energies, we tap into the perceptions that make us feel lighter. Harmony is created in the body. Tapping into the super-consciousness, we can replace the painful cell receptors with ones that crave experiences of wealth, happiness, and peace.

It is time to set the unconscious wounds down. It's time to let them go and be free of their control. As we hold on to our pain and wounds through heavy emotions, these emotions hold onto us. Just for the moment, imagine what it might be like to put this weight down, off to the side. It may be something that has been carried around for a long time, and it is heavy.

Anger is a hot rock we pick up to throw at someone to hurt them back. As we continue to cling to the rage or resentment, it burns within us. It consumes our vitality and life force. It eats away at us. It distracts us from being happy, loving, and joyful. It also affects everyone around us.

Take a moment to take a deep breath.
Hold it for the count of five.
Exhale this breath gently and easily.
Take another deep breath and as it is released, breathe out,
discharging tension, thoughts, and any busyness of the day.
Relax.
Breathe.
Trust.

We surrender to all that we do not know.
We let go, and we let God.

Now we are able to allow ourselves
to receive the grace of forgiveness.

We can begin with these steps and repeat them to ourselves until
we are up to doing deeper healing and forgiveness if needed.
Remember, we are speaking directly to our unconscious mind. It is
this part of the mind that everything we see, feel, and experience
comes from. As we heal ourselves, the unconscious self, the world
around us "cannot, not change" in response to our healing.

These are the basic steps of Ho'oponopono:

1. I am sorry.
2. Please forgive me.
3. Thank you.
4. I love you.

Bring to mind who or what you want to forgive.

Say these four lines in order and with intention.

Continue to repeat these statements until you feel a shift
and the peace this prayer promises.

An even gentler approach is to randomly repeat the statements
a few times throughout the day.

Practicing the Ho'oponopono allows you to become aware of your inner child and the suffering this small being may be feeling. Through this forgiveness practice, we show compassion to ourselves and our inner child.

²For the deeper Ho'oponopono steps, the prayer Dr. Len said, and much more information, read *Zero Limits*. Or, find a trained and certified Ho'oponopono practitioner. More information is available on Ho'oponopono websites.

³*The Secret*, directed by Drew Heriot, Prime Time Productions, 2006

16

The Dream We Dream

My whole world opened up when I learned about Ho'oponopono and the amazing work of Dr. Ihaleakala Hew Len. I then delved even deeper into understanding forgiveness and its unlimited power to heal. I studied HeartMath and living from our heart center.

The electromagnetic field emitting from the heart is up to five thousand times stronger than that of the brain! The heart is the first organ to develop and function in a fetus. The heart's electromagnetic field helps develop the other organs and the fetus. The heart also helps develop the brain!! There is a brain within the heart.

When the neural pathways in our solar plexus, heart, and pre-frontal cortex (which regulates decision-making and emotional processing) communicate effectively, we experience a state of flow- heart and mind coherence. When we are in this flow, we are open to receiving answers, wisdom, and guidance from our intuition.

When the electromagnetic fields of the heart, brain, and solar plexus are aligned, we access higher guidance. Everyone is capable of receiving whispers from the Ancient Ones.

After studying *The Disappearance of the Universe* by Gary Genard, I was ready to really learn about the teachings of *A Course In Miracles*[4].

ACIM opened my mind and heart even more, bringing me to an exalted awareness of so many answers and understandings! Being a large volume of higher-thought information and a spiritual self-study program to digest and comprehend, ACIM is usually studied in a group with a certified instructor for over a year. Through a non-dualistic perspective, it teaches forgiveness, inner peace, and the illusion of separation. ACIM emphasizes that love is the only reality, while fear and guilt are illusions that can be undone through a shift in perception. Similarly, many indigenous cultures describe our existence as the dream we are all dreaming together.

We think we are separate from the One; however, in reality, we have not left the peace of God. It is only in our minds that we dream the dreams of this reality and our experiences here.

As we become aware of our dreams, and become aware we are dreaming within a dream, we can then control and navigate through our dreams while our body sleeps. Conscious dreaming can assist us in doing the same in our assumed waking state. This is another tool to help us take back our lives. As you are in your dream of your life experiences as your brain knows it, imagine being a lucid dreamer. A lucid dreamer is aware they are in a dream and dreaming. The lucid dreamer begins to learn how to maneuver within the dream world. Eventually, the lucid dreamer becomes proficient at orchestrating the dream.

Forgiveness is the maneuvering tool in our lives.

A lucid dream can be used as a safe place to practice forgiveness when it seems too difficult to accomplish in waking life. Everything we see outside of ourselves reflects what is going on within us. Conflicts, wars, the stress on the news, good, bad, and indifferent are all projected from within ourselves to the outside to someone or something else. By asking our higher power to help with forgiving what we perceive to see, we begin to heal ourselves and the illusion that we are separate from Source. We are not separate. The mind simply sees the illusion that we are.

Problems, drama, stress, disease, pain, and suffering distract us from who we truly are as each of them draws us away from Source. When we forgive, we maneuver ourselves to peace. When we feel peace, we are feeling what it is like to be one again. Our life becomes easier. Our life begins to transition into a tranquil existence. There is less stress. There is more happiness. And miraculously, others change because we have changed.

As we help ourselves we are helping others.
As we help others we are helping ourselves.

Around eight years old, I began asking from my heart to "help me to help others as I help myself. Help me to help myself as I help others." This came into my mind as a child, and it became my mantra throughout life. It plays in the back of my mind throughout the day. I knew my purpose in coming to earth was to make a difference for the better in the ways that I could.

With this, please know that we must become our own first priority. As we heal the pain and fear within us, we literally heal the
world. What is inward is reflected outward. Understanding all of this
is not needed. We just do the steps of forgiveness in the best way that
we can. Practicing forgiveness is the way out of pain and the way
home to peace. This book is to share what helped me to heal and find
peace.

I honor you on your journey as we each navigate struggle in our
lives. The way out is to move through it. Move through it and come
out the other side whole and stronger than before. Forgiveness led me
through and out to the other side to find peace, healing, and empowerment.

According to the teachings of *A Course In Miracles*, all discord is
cleverly disguised as other people, places, and things, outside of ourselves. If we are distracted by what we think or feel someone else is
doing or has done, then we can avoid looking inward. We can avoid
having to face the pain within. We each seek acceptance. We each
want to know we are whole, complete, and perfect. As much as a
stretch this may seem to be. Whole, complete, and perfect is the reality of what each and every one of us is.

How can this be with the horrible crimes and things that happen?
People are acting out of character from how they are truly created.
They are coming from a place of a false identity. The further away
from their center (Source) the more discord and chaos they will find
themselves in. They are lost within the dream, taken over by their unconscious guilt, shame, and fear, driven by an ego that is out of its
mind with insanity.

**Our Prime Creator/God is love and only love. The ways of the
world are of the insane mind fearing it has left God.**

Everything we see outside of ourselves is really going on within
one's mind. The ego has us in an illusion that there are billions of sep-

arate bodies outside of ourselves. Judging and condemning does seem to temporarily alleviate some of the pain we might feel. What it is really doing is pulling us back into the false illusion of something else being the problem and placing the blame elsewhere.

[4]*A Course in Miracles* (New York: Foundation for Inner Peace, 1976) was written by Helen Schucman with transcription assistance by William Thetford. Schucman claimed to receive it through inner dictation from an inner voice she identified as Jesus Christ, with Thetford providing essential support in the process.

17

Letting Go of Our Stuff

Writing our feelings out on paper initiates breakthroughs. Writing is a technique that releases the energetic emotional muck around the heart so we are open to higher guidance. It works even if someone is depressed or has been detached from their feelings for a long time.

Begin with anything. Just start writing. Write what is on your mind, and what is stirring in that thinking machine. What feelings are there or not? What else do you notice? Write that down, too. Write any colors, symbols, or distractions that appear in your thoughts on that piece of paper. Let the pen or pencil be the instrument that connects deep within, drawing out from within. Allow the words to flow. Release the anger, the hurt, the pain, the frustrations, any resentment, and the injustice of it all. Release any emotions onto the paper. Let it all flow out onto that paper.

The paper soaks up the emotions and removes their negative charges. Writing is a big step in releasing what is pent up within us. It makes us feel lighter, opening our hearts and freeing us of the emotions that have caused discomfort.

Journaling our thoughts and feelings releases the toxins attached to deep-held emotions.

In dealing with someone who has harmed us or we feel hurt by, we can again imagine this person standing in front of us as a three or four-year-old child. We are simply finding a way to help us feel better. We are not excusing anything. This is for us and not about them.

The HeartSight Technique

Sit silently in a space without distractions. Take a deep, cleansing breath and close your eyes.

Close your eyes and **imagine this child expressing their deepest, heartfelt sorrow and regret for the hurt they caused.** See them expressing sincere remorse as they explain why they did what they did. They may not know why.

Recognize the torment the child has within themselves.

Bring to mind who or what you love. Feel this love. Bring it fully into your heart and mind until you smile. Focus on your heart and your breathing until you feel this love welling in your heart area. Allow this joyful love to circulate throughout your entire body.

Place your hand on your heart and spend a few minutes here, breathing and focusing on your heart. This helps to collapse and replace the neural pathway associated with the pain within the emotional body. It can then create a new neural pathway associated with pleasant emotions. We have over seventy trillion cells in our bodies. Each cell is saturated with this joyful love we are feeling as we continue to think of who and what we love that brings an instant smile to our faces.

Without needing understanding or really knowing why or how, **appreciate the child's deep remorse,** keeping your heart on the child and filled with compassion.

Allow yourself to trust and accept that this child is coming from a sincere place in their heart in asking our forgiveness. By accepting their apology, you are releasing the emotional hold it has had on you. You are creating a mental, emotional, physical, spiritual, and energetic liberation.

Imagine holding a very large pair of scissors or a sword. Cut the energetic ties between you and this person in your imagination. This cuts the negative experiences associated with them. (You can do this again at any time, anywhere to dissolve energetic cords between someone or something.)

Now, you will **replace the stuff you just released with soothing, restorative, and healing energy.** Imagine a beautiful, soft violet light. Allow this light to flow deep within, filling every space everywhere inside the emotional body, the energy body, the mental body, the physical body, and the etheric body.

Take a few moments to feel or **sense the calmness, as this comforting violet light** flows throughout each and every one of the body's cells, completely filling it up.

Call in understanding from the innate wisdom of life to come to you now. This supports you in the rational aspects of what you released, the peace received, and the healing taking place.

Ask to receive the blessing and gift from this experience.

By releasing with compassion what someone has done to harm us, we release their hold on us, setting us free. We can then realize we have actually overcome this experience now. We have taken back our lives!

As your pain lessens, you'll experience a growth in compassion and love for your inner child.

There is a gift and blessing in everything we experience in life. Often, the most amazing gifts and blessings come from the worst experiences. Again, releasing the damage and the pain an experience caused does not condone any actions, say it was okay in any way, or discount any suffering we have gone through. It is about freeing us from any further need to be connected to the experience, the person, and the baggage. It is about receiving peace, healing inner injuries, and receiving the blessing of becoming empowered and stronger because of what happened.

It is about taking back our lives!

18

Lucid Dreaming - A Powerful Tool

Lucid dreaming is being aware that we are dreaming, while we are dreaming. Even more than this, it is taking control of the direction of our dreams!

The term "lucid dreaming" was first coined by Frederik van Eeden, a Dutch psychiatrist and writer, in 1913. In his paper "A Study of Dreams", he used the term "lucid" to describe dreams in which the dreamer is aware that they are dreaming.

Besides being so fascinating, lucid dreaming can be very valuable in our lives. As many theories and beliefs point to, we are all of one mind, seeing ourselves as many individuals. We are dreaming our entire existence. We are dreaming when we sleep, and we continue to dream the dream when we perceive ourselves to be awake.

Lucid dreaming gets our mind to understand how it can consciously direct our lives as we choose. Remember, thoughts are physical things. Thoughts and emotions are powerful manifesting devices. It is of the utmost importance to be the driver of our vehicle. Our body being the vehicle.

So, while we are here, learning and growing and raising our vibrations and that of our planet, let us utilize the power tool of lucid dreaming. Let's allow it to make a huge impact on our lives. Approximately one-third of our lives is spent sleeping. This equates to between twenty-five to thirty years in an average life span. About twenty-five percent of our sleep time is spent dreaming.

Lucid dreamers are known to increase this normal dream time to an astonishing eighteen years of productive use time! We can only imagine how we could make use of those years otherwise just spent dreaming.

I know several lucid dreamers and I am one, as well. One is a scientist and inventor who utilizes his sleep time to work out formulas and problems regarding his inventions and work. He wakes up each morning with the answers to his questions. Every scenario is worked out, resulting in having the best solution to his problem... even advanced math problems he is not good with.

It began when he had nightmares as a child. In his nightmares, he was a small dot with a larger dot chasing him. He was aware it was a dream while he was dreaming, however, he always woke up terrified, with his heart racing. He saw a psychologist who guided him to imagine his dreams on a television to help with these nightmares. This child learned to change the channel to something else when the nightmare began. After a while, he became very good at deciding what he wanted to do in his dreams. As a teenager, the young man became an avid inventor.

What work, relationship, or health-related challenges could we solve by using our extra years of sleep for problem-solving? A woman I knew used lucid dreaming to help heal a painful shoulder she had long been dealing with. Another friend uses her lucid dreams to learn the meaning of her dream symbols and synchronistic messages she receives in her daily life. Lucid dreaming reveals what her unconscious mind is telling her. She gets answers to her deepest questions and insight into what she can shift so that she is in control of her life. She also learned to stand up to her fears by gaining knowledge about her dreamtime metaphoric messages while lucid dreaming.

And still another person I know well- an intuitive clairvoyant since birth- gets impressions about her past lives. She travels in her dreamtime to relive those past lives and get clarity on questions she has about them. If you believe in past lives, have you ever thought of exploring any of them?

Can health issues be healed in dream time? We could call in a specialist to meet with us in our dreams. Can relationship issues be solved? We can call upon the higher self of the other person to converse with them from a higher perspective. Another user of lucid dreaming spontaneously went lucid late one night at a restaurant while sitting near a stranger. She went into a higher dimension where she and the stranger were happily laughing while concocting a plan to get the two of them together in the third dimension. Eighteen months later, they met again, and they've been together for nearly two decades now.

Before I met my husband, Mike, I spent time with my idea of the man of my dreams while lucid dreaming. Until he showed up, I met with my image of him in my lucid dream state. I knew what his energy felt like before we met. I would feel this energy from time to time when I was awake, also.

Do you have loved ones you would like to see more often? Maybe loved ones who have passed on or who live far away- even those you have not met that you would like to get to know? It is often believed that our deceased loved ones visit us in our dreams. Because we are dreaming, it is much easier to meet with them. Most people would be scared or upset to see their loved ones who have passed on during their waking time.

Lucid dreaming can be a lot of fun. We can mastermind in our lucid dreams and meet the great minds of history. We can meet the authors of our favorite books, spend time with loved ones, and explore different dimensions of ourselves. I have even heard of and read about people using their lucid dreams to time travel and explore alternate universes, and to meet advanced intelligent beings. They time-travel in their dreams, as did the woman who revisits her past lives. And still others join in other people's dreams and vice versa. I have heard from married couples who often share the same dream.

How about using lucid dreams to visit the future? By setting clear intentions before sleep, you could explore potential outcomes, gain insights, or receive symbolic messages about what lies ahead. Lucid dreaming allows access to deeper intuition, creativity, and unconscious wisdom, making it a powerful tool for envisioning possibilities and guiding real-life decisions.

If some of this is a bit too wild, simply consider being aware of dreams while dreaming. As I previously suggested, a lucid dream can be used as a safe place to practice forgiveness when it seems too difficult to accomplish in our waking life. This brings to mind the incredible inventions and accomplishments that we have had throughout history. It makes sense that they certainly could have originated from lucid dreamers who were masterful with their lucid dream time.

Think of the pyramids and some of the other marvels we have in our world. Where did this amazing knowledge come from, and how were those things communicated? A higher intelligence of some sort from somewhere played a big part in these. I have also read about the giants living at that time, building the pyramids. This is, however, another topic for another book. One of the greatest minds, Einstein, often referred to his lucid dreams in his writings. When some of the greatest minds of our world refer to their lucid dreams, it adds another level of validity.

If we would like to improve our capability at something, such as golf or tennis for instance, we can improve our skills while we are lucid. Because of the vivid imagery and the physiological nature of REM sleep, it is ideal for establishing neural patterns without actual movement. It's been proven that we can become physically stronger with mental training, i.e., the Olympic athletes who go through the entire training in their minds and also physically train. They always far excel over the athletes who only train physically. I think this is amazing information. The possibilities can be unlimited! We can pretty much do whatever we want without the limits and restrictions that are common in our waking hours. Restraints such as gravity, time, distance, or even what someone else may think.

What about changing negative thinking into positive thinking with our lucid dreaming time? Since dreams reflect our unconscious patterns, we can use lucid dreaming to rewire limiting beliefs, practice affirmations, and reinforce a more empowering mindset. How about using our dream time to focus on manifesting the things we would like to see show up in our waking life? By visualizing our desires in a lucid state, we align our energy with our intentions, making it easier to attract them into reality.

First of all, it's important to know that we do dream. We can ask ourselves if we have ever found ourselves dreaming or remembering a part of a dream. We may not be aware that we dream, or we might not remember our dreams. Be assured, we do indeed dream; even if we are not aware of it or if we do not recall our dreams.

Dreaming is a sequence of mental images which occur during sleep. It is usually a mixture of real events and imaginary characters, images, symbols, colors, and places. It is as natural and necessary a function as eating, drinking water, and breathing. The mind works out issues as we are sleeping through dreaming.

We are given messages through our dreams from our unconscious mind that can be used to help us in our waking life. In a lucid dream, we can learn how to decide to take control and direct the way we are going, even when we feel lost. With learning to lucid dream, realize that many people have done this before us. It is a learnable skill and that's encouraging! And, there are a variety of techniques available for inducing lucid dreams.

This is my conclusion from all of the various research and studies done through the years on lucid dreaming, i.e., Stephen LaBerge, founder of the Lucidity Institute, conducted significant research on lucid dreaming, including collaborations with researchers at Stanford University, among many others. Lucid dreaming is a step-by-step process that can be learned just as we learned to walk before we learned to run.

Think back to a challenging step-by-step process, where you spent a lot of time crawling before you walked: mastering a musical instrument or a new language, learning the ropes at a new job, recovering from a setback, or preparing that perfect dinner that the entire family loves. Excelling at these tasks took development just as it does with lucid dreaming. You put in much effort to learn how to crawl, and with crawling, you felt like you were going places. You put in more effort to learn how to run- with running, you could go to more places and faster. The effort that you put into lucid dreaming gets stored in the unconscious mind, and sooner than you know it, you're traveling faster than the speed of light.

With each step of the way in lucid dreaming, we can track our progress and prove to ourselves that we are getting there. Just as we did when we first were able to turn ourselves over in our crib, to get ourselves into a position to begin moving forward, and then to finally start crawling. How long can we imagine, as an infant, we gazed at the vast array of colors and objects, until finally being able to focus in on things and people's faces? Then, to focus on our hands? How long did we gaze at our hands, before we wondered what they were and how they could be used? It is the same with lucid dreaming and forgiveness. They are step-by-step processes, which we can learn.

19

Dream Signs

Dream Signs are odd things and occurrences in our dreams. Since a base goal of lucid dreaming is to be aware that we are dreaming while it's happening, we can use a Dream Sign to trigger us into lucid awareness. Realizing a Dream Sign while sleeping can cause us to immediately become lucid. Being aware of these Dream Signs will set your intention to look for them while sleeping to trigger lucidity.

**These are a few Dream Signs to look for
to tell that you are dreaming:**

• **Checking a Clock:** Seeing a clock, the digital time will change, hands will shift, or the clock will disappear when you look away and back again in a dream. Look at the clock, then turn away and look at the clock again.

• **Reading Words on a Page:** Looking at words on a page is similar to a clock. Looking away and then back to the page can cause the words, the page, or the book to change or disappear in a dream.

• **Flipping a Light Switch:** Normally, light switches do not work in a dream. Try flipping it on or off if you see one while sleeping.

• **Looking Into a Mirror:** Your reflection will usually be blurry in a dream, or you will see yourself reflected as a different person, either known or unknown to you. Look into the mirror if you see one while sleeping.

• **Holding Your Nose Closed while Breathing**: With your mouth shut, close your nose with your fingers. You can breathe in a dream while doing this.

• **Glancing at your hands:** Normally, in a dream, you will see more or fewer fingers or thumbs on your hand, or your hands do not seem to be your hands in some odd way.

• **Jumping in the air:** You are usually able to fly in dreams when you jump up or dart forward. Try taking a leap.

• **Poking yourself:** In a dream, your flesh might be more elastic than in real life. Pull, poke, or stretch your skin to see if it's cartoonish or elastic, which ensures you're dreaming.

• **Biting yourself:** In a dream, you might not feel the pain of the bite.

• **Leaning against a wall:** In dreams, you will usually fall through walls when you lean on them.

Techniques To Help You Lucid Dream:

1. Before drifting off to sleep, tell yourself several times that you will wake up immediately when you think or say, "I want to wake up now!"

2. Set your intention to physically roll over in bed while you are asleep and dreaming. You will use rolling over in bed to change the direction of your lucid dream when you want your dream to change. This starts the process of gaining control of the direction of your dreams.

3. Spinning in your lucid dream. When you are lucid, spin around a few times. Spinning can cause your lucid dream to continue longer. You will be in a different location when you come out of the spin, so expect this to avoid being startled, which might wake you up.

Once you are comfortable with and mastering being lucid, you can then set an intention to accomplish before drifting off to sleep. Remember to be persistent in learning and applying these techniques. Continue to be insistent with your unconscious mind. It exists to serve and protect you. You are teaching it how to follow your lead, and you are learning yourself.

More About Lucid Dreamers

I personally interviewed the lucid dreamers I mentioned in this book for the paper I wrote on "Modeling." This paper was part of the criteria for my NLP Master Practitioner training. We each chose a topic that interested us and then explained the steps and methods, which could be followed (modeled) to reach success.

The inventor (I'll call him Dave) from the last chapter had a much more interesting story than I explained. As a teen, Dave created a television with dials and seven pleasant-to-watch channels in his dreams so he could change the channel when he found himself in a nightmare. When in a night terror, in his lucid dream, he consciously changed the channel. This was a wonderful change for him. Finally, Dave had peace!

However, in the beginning, Dave had difficulty turning the channels. So, he devised a method of holding onto the television dial while turning himself over physically in his bed, while asleep. He realized this changed the direction of his lucid dreams, placing him into a different scene.

Dave had a passion for designing trucks and trains, as well as re-powering trucks. He meticulously documented every aspect of the process- analyzing challenges, logging details, writing reports, and creating sketches and technical drawings. Most of his problem-solving and design innovations took place in his lucid dreams, where he even explored market demands for his ideas.

Before going to bed each night, he set his intention on what he needed to figure out. The problem or questions were worked out while he slept and in his lucid dreams. He woke up in the morning with the answers and all the countless scenarios worked out with the best plan presented to him

Years later, as a career inventor, Dave had one of his many incredible breakthroughs using lucid dreaming. He had worked for six years on integrating watercraft hydrofoils with other technologies. At a critical juncture, he needed input from a physicist but couldn't efficiently explain his six years' worth of data and findings. Yet, with lucid dreaming, where he was often directed to wake up and record the information being given, he learned which material was pertinent out of all the volumes of documents, data, and mathematical equations involving hydrofoil dynamics, fluid mechanics, and material properties. Dave then defined the problem in detail in a two-page letter to the physicist. The information he received through lucid dreaming led to six years of work being whittled down into two pertinent pages that led to his success!

In lucid dreams, Dave was frequently led to research something that led him to uncover fascinating and significant information he was not looking for. As I mentioned earlier, he obtained answers to high-level math formulas, even though he was not good with math. He always woke up with the answers he needed. Such as the time he went to sleep with a propulsion system problem and was given the conclusion to it in the morning. He told me, "I look forward to going to sleep. I get things done. Life continues to improve, and I have less anxiety. It is a very productive thing."

Then again, there was the woman who faced her fears while dreaming. She would meditate on her question during the day and set her intention to get the answer before going to sleep. She regularly received the answers in her dreams, in the morning, or later the next day. Before learning how to direct her lucid dreams, she learned to wake herself up if she wanted to get out of the dream. From this, she developed a way to help herself when having night terrors and being chased.

Typically, something horrifying would chase her. Then suddenly, from somewhere in her unconscious, came a magical ink. She learned that the best way to extract herself from the night terrors was to face what was chasing her and throw the magical ink on it. This dissipated the terror and incapacitated the thing intimidating her. She then asked it why it was chasing her and what message it had for her. When she received the answers, she threw more of the ink on it, causing it to disappear. Later, she was able to change it into something sweet like a bunny. Eventually, she could simply tell it to leave, and it would disappear.

One of the first times I realized I was lucid in my dreams was when I was dealing with a dark force that had intentions of taking over my life force. I would have loved to have known about the magic ink back then. I was about fourteen and I found myself being intimidated by a huge, dark, very threatening force. It commanded me to allow it to take over my being, continuing to threaten me with its power and capability to do this.

Even though I felt intimidated and afraid, I stood up to it in my lucid dream. I told it, "I know your power is just an illusion of real power. I know I am dreaming, so you cannot take me over!" I knew somehow that the more powerful it appeared to be, the closer it was to its last display of this intimidating, false power. It was an illusion of power. I continued to hold onto my convictions, to stand up to it, although it was extremely intimidating, and it continued to attempt to terrify me into submission. I finally woke up and realized that it was a dream and that the dark force did not have any power over me.

I had this exact dream twice. A dark force tried to overpower me, but I stood my ground, declaring, "I know I am dreaming. This is a dream!" Yet, between the two dreams, I woke up several times in the middle of the night, feeling an eerie presence lingering over me. A supernatural shadow bore down on my upper body, leaving me paralyzed. The first two times, it vanished as soon as I managed to move my arms and legs. But the third time, the pressure intensified, pinning me down. I felt an overwhelming, dense darkness. It took longer for me to even twitch a finger, and only then did the presence finally dissipate. (After a lifetime of contemplation and memory retrieval, I realized that Dad had these experiences even if he wasn't fully cognizant of them. I know that it was this dark force that hit me. Forgiving my father not only saved me, it freed me and my family from the grip of these dark forces.)

In the second lucid dream, as it was in the process of overpowering me, I told it, "I know your power is an illusion and not real. I know the bigger the display of your power to be able to take me over, the closer you are to the grand finale of this illusion." As I was seemingly being overpowered in the dream, I was also waking up. I thought and spoke simultaneously, "In the name of Jesus and the White Light, NO!" The force began to dissipate as my voice changed to a very deep, long "Noooooooooooo." I was completely awake at that time, with the deep "Noooooooooooo" coming out of me.

I got out of bed. I realized it had not taken me over. It was only a scary, intensely intimidating illusion of something doing its best to deceive me. After that, it did not come back. Even though I felt the after-effects of that nightmare lucid dream, I managed to wake myself up.

I find it amazing that I knew how to handle whatever this force was. I had an inner knowing telling me it was an illusion of power, and I had the strength and the courage to stand up to it.

Over and beyond fear and intimidation is peace that we are always connected to. From within that peace came the whispers from the Ancient Ones. Even in moments of seemingly grand confusion, you can listen to your heart and receive the Ancient Ones' messages.

From that time forward, if I sense an uncomfortable presence, I tell it to leave and call in the angels to fill the room with Divine energy. I also learned how to energetically and physically clear the energy in my entire home. I routinely do an energetic cleansing before I go to sleep at night. This includes physically cleaning my home, taking a salt bath or placing my feet in running water, and using the spirit of something like palo santo to dissipate all negative charges within my home.

If I find myself in an unpleasant dream or a nightmare, I simply decide to wake up, and I do. I forgive myself for whatever is within me that has attracted such a presence. I do the Ho'oponopono and thank the Ancient Ones for their presence with the Earth People.

I have always found it very intriguing, the lyrics "life is but a dream" in the following song:

"Row, row, row your boat, gently down the stream.
Merrily, merrily, merrily, merrily...
Life is but a dream."
~ *Eliphalet Oram Lyte in 1881*

Resources

Christopher Howard, MNLP, MTD, MH.t: NLP Classes. Los Angeles, CA.

Jane Lake, Ph.D. Clinical Hypnotherapy. Friend, teacher, and mentor. I was blessed to know her. Canyon Lake, CA.

Ho'oponopono: More information and origin: Hawaiian Kahuna Morrnah Nalamaku Simeona. https://hooponoponomiracle.com/ho-oponopono-technique/

Dr. Ihaleakala Hew Len: Information on Dr.Hew Len: https://discover.hubpages.com/religion-philosophy/How-Dr-Hew-Len-healed-a-ward-of-mentally-ill-criminals-with-Hooponopono

Matt Brauning, MNLP, MTD, MH.t. Evolution Seminars: NLP, Hypnotherapy, and Hypnosis training. Orange County, Ca.

Michael Mirdad, Minister. The Global Center of Christ Consciousness: Teacher and mentor. A.C.I.M, numerous classes and trainings. I was also a chaplain. Sedona, AZ.

Nicholas Rave, MNLP, MTD, MH.t. Rave Seminars: NLP Master, Hypnotherapy, and Hypnosis training. Orange County, CA. Teacher and mentor.

Pamela Harper, RN, CCH, CAC: One of my first mentors and teachers. Clinical Hypnotherapy, N.L.P., first level Reiki, addiction counselor, and life coach training, many other classes. San Clemente, CA.

Rev. Deborah Durrough, Registered Reiki Master and Karuna Reiki® Master Instructor: Friend and instructor. Usui Reiki Master and Karuna Reki ®Master trainings and a multitude of other classes. Corona, CA.

BOOKS:

Arntz, W., Chasse, B., & Vincente, M. (2005) *What the Bleep Do We Know?* Deerfield Beach, FL: Heath Communications.

Bruce, A. (2005) *Beyond the Bleep.* NY, NY: The Disinformation Company.

Gawan, S. (1978) *Creative Visualization: Use the power of your imagination to create what you want in your life.* Novato, CA: Nataraj Publishing.

Hay, L. (2004) *You Can Heal Your Life*. Carlsbad, CA: Hay House.

Renard, G. (2004) *The Disappearance of the Universe*. Carlsbad, CA: Hay House.

Schucman, H. (1976) *A Course in Miracles*. Mill Valley, CA: Foundation for Inner Peace.

Tolle, E. (1999) *The Power of Now: A guide to spiritual enlightenment*. Novato, CA: Namaste Publishing.

Vitale, J., & Len, I. H. (2007) *Zero Limits: The Hawaiian system for wealth, health, peace, & more.* Hoboken, NJ:

John Wiley & Sons. Walsch, N. D. (1998) *The Little Soul and the Sun*. Hampton Roads Publishing

INFLUENCERS:

"Creative Visualization" by Shakti Gawain

"Zero Limits" by Joe Vitale and Ihaleakala Hew Len, Ph.D.

David Icke www.davidicke.com More information on YouTube.

Isabella Greene www.Isabellagreene.com Leaving the simulation. More information on YouTube videos and books. 'Leaving the simulation' training.

Additional Reading and Videos

Desiderata from The Poems of Max Ehrmann

A New Earth by Eckhart Tolle

Ask And It Is Given by Ester and Jerry Hicks

Fearless by Steve Chandler

Loving What Is by Byron Katie

Think And Grow Rich by Napoleon Hill

Living The Science of Mind by Ernest Holmes

The Seven Spiritual Laws of Success by Deepak Chopra

The Four Agreements by Don Miguel Ruiz

The Four Agreements Companion Book by Don Miguel Ruiz

VIDEOS:

"What The Bleep Do We Know?" William Arntz, Betsy Chasse, and Mark Vincente

"Beyond the Bleep" Alexander Bruce

"Remember Who You Are" David Icke

"This Will Absolutely Blow Your Mind" David Icke

"The Matrix" All of the original movies

Pass It On Book Series

Your Journey Doesn't End Here... *Whispers from the Ancient Ones* is the second of 144 books in the **'Pass It On'** series. Each story unlocks new insights from life's most profound challenges. By sharing in the wisdom of others, you can find deeper understanding and re-newed strength for your path. Check out these published or upcoming titles.

OUR HEARTSONG - Published - Be swept away into the heart of life, which is unconditional love. Experience peace and an influx of faith simply by reading these heart-truths to lift your vibration and bring higher possibilities into your awareness. (W. Werner)

TRUCKIN' THROUGH TWO REALITIES -A schizo-phrenic truck driver's journey through two realities to retrieve the inherent wisdom we were born with. (A. Wessel)

THE RUNWAY RUNAWAY- A memoir of a destitute and abused Brazilian street child who, against all odds, followed God's bread-crumbs with unwavering faith- ultimately rising from hardship to grace the European runways of top designers like Versace. (W. Lima)

THE BOOT- An opera singer's rebellious journey: From Mor-monism to Namaste (Violet Sage)

IN EVERY SOUL IS A SONG – PART I, THE FIRST DIMEN-SION- Multi-dimensional healing and attuning the physical to the Higher Self- experience gained from a near-death-experience to uplift every aspect of life (Rev. M. Lucas)

CAPRIS-CORN- The wisdom and karmic imprint of Capricorn in astrology (Rev. F.D. James)

About the Author

E. C. Sanders is a multi-published author, freelance editor, and public speaker. She is board-certified as a Neuro Linguistic Programming Master, a Clinical Hypnotherapist, Holistic Nutritionist, and a Usui and Karuna Reiki Master. She is additionally certified in advanced levels of Pranic Healing, Deeksha Oneness, and Avesa Healing. Now retired, she formerly taught classes on empowerment, healing through forgiveness, nutrition, and health.

E.C. is an empath and psychically gifted. Some of her fondest memories are swimming with wild dolphins in Hawaii and California during the years she lived there. She has been an ethical vegan vegetarian since 1970. E.C. lives in Hot Springs Village, Arkansas, with her best friend and beloved husband, Mike.